GRAND AND BROADWAY-1910

This specially bound edition of
THE VANISHED SPLENDOR II
is limited to 200 numbered, signed
copies of which 160 are for sale.

This is number ___44___

THE VANISHED SPLENDOR II

A POSTCARD ALBUM OF OKLAHOMA CITY

By Jim Edwards and Hal Ottaway

Mitchell Oliphant
Historical and Editorial Consultant

ABALACHE BOOK SHOP PUBLISHING CO.
311 South Klein
Oklahoma City, Oklahoma 73108
1983

(COVER)

This is a 1950 view of Oklahoma City's once proud and flourishing Main Street, looking west from Broadway. **Of special significance is the fact that none of the buildings, businesses, or colorful neon signs shown in this view exist today!** This complete destruction of the heart of Oklahoma City was carried out in the name of Urban Renewal.

Among the well remembered merchants was W. J. Pettee, who made the run in 1889, opened his first hardware store on West Main soon thereafter, and worked out of a tent. Later a frame building was erected, followed in 1906 by the five-story brick structure at 121-123 West Main.

Rector's Book Store, formerly known as Stevenson's, was next door east of Pettee's. By 1973, it had relocated to the Mayfair Shopping Center at Fiftieth and North May. For the last three decades Rector's has been owned and operated by the Vater family.

INTRODUCTION

Unlike the hobbies of philately and numismatics, where every single stamp and coin is known and catalogued, one of the appeals of being a deltiologist, or postcard collector, is that the element of adventure is always present. New discoveries are constantly being made by both novice and advanced collectors. This has been proven time and again when people wrote or phoned to tell of postcards in their collections or in albums that parents or grandparents had given them, providing leads that have uncovered heretofore unknown businesses and scenes. Through the generosity of many people this publication has been made possible. The authors believe it is important to bring these postcards together so that this visual aspect of Oklahoma City history might be more complete and the images be preserved and remembered.

Assuming that those who bought or were given **The Vanished Splendor** might want this companion volume, too, we have continued the numbering system and a combined index for both volumes is at the end of this work. We hope that the index will make the two volume set more useful for reading pleasure and reference in the home and library.

The process of selecting images for these books seems to interest readers, and it should be stated that we wish that every memory would have been available on a postcard; but this is not always the case. Had they been available we would have featured Bishop's Restaurant, the Midwest and Liberty Theatres, Kaiser's Ice Cream Store, Webster High School, Capitol Hill High School, and other well known city landmarks. Should these views be discovered as postcards, the authors would be pleased to see them.

The Vanished Splendor II is a postcard album of Oklahoma City from before statehood through and including the 1950's: six decades of achievement and growth, and, along the way, a lot of changes. Shown in all their splendor are the favorite drive-in, the car dealership where you, a friend, or a relative bought their first car, or perhaps the restaurant where you and your family attended a birthday or special celebration. We include homes, schools, churches, places of entertainment and amusement, the early-day bird men who flew in open planes (and later carried the first air mail from Oklahoma City) ... something to stimulate every reader's memory. In some way nearly everyone's life has been touched by these historic images, and it is our hope that you will enjoy your journey back in time to the days of **The Vanished Splendor II.**

We were fortunate to have continuity with the first book through the expert assistance of Mitchell Oliphant of Oklahoma City. Mitchell's knowledge of the area never ceases to be amazing. His untiring efforts and encouragement have helped to make both of these volumes a reality.

Lastly, we appreciate the forbearance of our respective families for all the times that we have not been available because we were working on the book. A special expression of appreciation goes to Ruth Edwards and Lucretia Ottaway for their understanding and assistance.

August, 1983   Hal Ottaway and Jim Edwards

181. This 1912 view looks south on Harvey across Main Street. The large structure on the left is the Security Building and the white one in the center background is the Goodholm Building, which later was the home of Miller Brothers Dry Goods (card no. 183) and, more recently, Sears, Roebuck and Company. To the right is The Mellon Company (card no. 51), easily identified by the portion of its illuminated sign which can be seen on top of the store. Later, this building housed Barth and Myer's clothing store and, still later, Rothschild's department store. At the far right is the distinctively narrow Majestic Building (card no. 42), a seven-story structure which was razed by explosives in April, 1977.

182. The viewpoint of this postcard is looking west on Main Street from Santa Fe, about 1907. T. D. Turner & Co., in the foreground on the right, was a wholesale fruit and produce business, specializing in confectionery goods and cigars. Kerfoot, Miller & Co., immediately west, dealt in staple dry goods from both domestic and foreign mills. The Bass and Harbour Furniture Co. was toward the end of the block. The building with the onion-like turret was the Masonic Temple (card no. 91). An earlier view (card no. 9) showing the north side of this block as seen from Broadway, makes an interesting comparison.

183. Photographers are seldom identified on postcards, but this card is marked "Pesha," the name of an image-maker who was more often associated with the work that he did in Ohio. Instead of lowering the camera lens and recording more foreground, a common practice of most photographers, Pesha chose to include the mosaic of trolley wires above the street. In doing this he showed an artistic flair which enhanced his work. The Miller Bros. Dry Goods Company to the right occupies the southeast corner of Grand and Harvey. Later the company moved to the multi-story Goodholm Building across the street, as noted in card no. 181.

184. Under a web of trolley wires, electric lights, and telephone wires, this view looks west from Santa Fe on Grand Avenue in late 1910 or early 1911. A construction shed in the right foreground is for work nearby. The Hotel Lawrence and Hotel Kingkade are completed, and further west the awnings on the arched windows of the three-story City Hall can be seen. The Baum and Colcord Buildings are in the distance. Handsome multi-globe street lights line both sides of the street, making it truly seem like a "great white way" after dark. The Doc & Bill Furniture Company, long a fixture in the community, is on the immediate left or south side of the street.

185. This mid-1920's street scene shows Main Street looking east from Robinson. On the far left is the Lee Office Building, later to become the Oil and Gas Building, but at this time housing the Liberty National Bank. Though extensively remodeled in recent years, this building still stands on the northeast corner of Main and Robinson. East of the Roach and Veazey Drug Company are two photo finishing stores: Classen Film Finishing and Pasevitch Photo Studio. The camera was an afforable luxury item and nearly everyone was taking "snaps" to send to friends and loved ones living elsewhere. Pettee's Hardware and the Tradesmens State Bank are easily recognized in the distance.

186. The viewpoint of this postcard, circa 1937, looks east on Main Street from Hudson. If North Broadway was "automobile alley" in the 1920's and 1930's, this, the 300 block of West Main, would certainly qualify as "shoe store alley." There were at least five such businesses on the block: Baker's, Paul's, Nissen's, Allens, and a Dr. Scholl's "Foot Comfort Station." This is not to mention the shoe departments of stores such as Street's, Penney's, and Kerr's, which were also located on the block.

187. This view looks south on Robinson at the Main Street intersection. A new $100,000 building was erected on the southwest corner for Katz Drug Store, which had its grand opening on November 21, 1936. Its advertising claimed: "A Katz customer not only can eat lunch and have a prescription filled, he can have his automobile decked out with accessories, his kitchen equipped with modern appliances, and his shoes half-soled." For opening day there were three full pages of get-acquainted bargains in the newspaper, such as alarm clocks for 63¢, a toasted bacon, lettuce & tomato sandwich with trimmings for 19¢, a pound of Katz certified coffee for 13¢, a 22 piece toy china tea set for 10¢, and more. A shopper's paradise! Generations grew up shopping at Katz. However, in the early 1960's the business closed, leaving a void downtown, and memories of a fine, old-time drug store.

188. With the First National Building (card no. 210) towering in the distance, this view looks east on Main from Harvey. Walgreen Drugs was located first in the Hales Building in the early 1930's, but moved to the corner location shown here at 229 West Main in June, 1938. In the recessed entrance area just off the street, Walgreen Drugs began selling fresh popcorn. Customers lined up, especially in the evening as they waited for their particular streetcar to take them home. Walgreen's sold an extra large sack of popcorn for just 10¢, and movie-goers would often stop at this corner for popcorn before going on to the theatre.

189. A motorist driving west in the 200 block of West Main in the early 1950's would have seen this veiw. The Hales Building is on the northwest corner to the right, and the John A. Brown store is in the middle of the same block. In 1915, Mr. Brown became a partner with his cousin Anson Rorabaugh and purchased the Brock Dry Goods Company. Later he purchased his cousin's interest and the store became known as the John A. Brown Company, "the nearest thing in Oklahoma City to Macy's." Additional stores were added through the years and today there are five major department stores and a specialty store in Norman. The business was acquired by the Dayton-Hudson Corporation in 1971. Every structure in this view has been demolished except the Hightower Building in the background.

190. The Criterion Theatre at 118 West Main was undoubtedly the ultimate in movie house extravagance. Built in 1921 at a cost of $700,000, it was an architectural triumph in terms of design. A point of pride was its organ which cost $25,000 and was considered at that time to be the largest in the state. Crystal chandeliers adorned the lobby, and thick velvet carpeting seemed to be everywhere. There were mural paintings, polished walnut wainscotting, and velour draperies — every detail seemed to exude luxury and comfort. Torn down in 1973, another victim of Urban Renewal, the Criterion is still remembered today almost reverently.

Robinson Street Looking North, Oklahoma City, Okla.

BRANIFF BUILDING, OKLAHOMA CITY, OKLA.

191. Just north of the Baum Building (card no. 48), where the Fidelity National Bank was located, was the State Theatre at 20 North Robinson. The State opened for business on March 5, 1937, with the feature, **When You're In Love,** starring Grace Moore and Cary Grant. The admission price was 10¢ for children, 20¢ for morning and early afternoon features, 25¢ for late afternoon, and 40¢ for nights and Sunday matinees. The nearby businesses were pleased to have the theatre as a neighbor since it added to the attraction of business in the downtown area.

192. Located at 324 North Robinson, the Braniff Building is presently part of the Kerr-McGee complex. The architectural firm of Layton, Hicks, and Forsyth designed this ten-story building, which was begun in 1922 and completed in 1923. For a time the city directory shows that the Layton firm was an occupant of the Braniff Building. It was constructed originally for Thomas E. Braniff, who needed the office space to house his successful insurance business. Later Mr. Braniff's entrepreneurial interests turned to the aviation industry, and he is famous as the founder of Braniff Airlines.

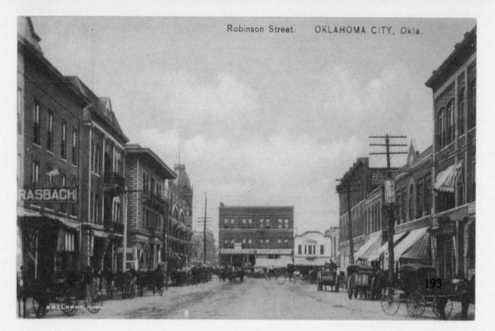

Robinson Street. OKLAHOMA CITY, Okla.

193. This circa 1908 view looks north in the unit block of South Robinson. The Rasbach Hotel on the left is distinguished in that it was once owned by Dr. Joseph Rolater (cards 142, 143). The interesting structure on the southwest corner of Grand and Robinson was the Farmers State Bank. The Land Office Building was on the northeast corner of Grand and Robinson, directly in front of the photographer. The right half of the Land was the home of the Doerr Candy Company. An interesting contrast can be seen by comparing this "before" view with that of card no. 4, its "after" counterpart. When the Land Building was razed it was replaced by the Baum Building (card no. 48).

Broadway. OKLAHOMA CITY, Okla.

194. Looking north on Broadway from Second Street, this 1907 street scene was selected because its wide-angle view placed several of the buildings that are well known individually in perspective with one another. To the left was the India Temple (card no. 92), constructed in 1902, containing the Palace Pharmacy on its ground floor and Coca-Cola and other advertising signs on its side. The seven-story white building further down the street was the Pioneer Telephone Building (card no. 85) at Third and Broadway. In the right foreground was the Threadgill Hotel (card no. 78), later renamed the Hotel Bristol. The Threadgill's electrified sign remained above Broadway for a number of years.

RENO AND ROBINSON, OKLAHOMA CITY, OKLA.

195. The Dunn Hotel, located at 207 South Robinson, was one of Oklahoma City's lesser known hotels, yet for more than half a century it occupied the southwest corner of Reno and Robinson. Opening its doors sometime in 1908, the hotel included Albert and John Varvel's Reno Pharmacy in a choice corner location on the ground floor. As the surrounding neighborhood gradually became a seamy area of flophouses, bars, and secondhand stores, the Dunn persevered, endeavoring to maintain its respectability. Demolished during the Urban Renewal era, the hotel has been mostly forgotten, and its site is now the location of a new Fred Jones Ford showroom.

196, 197 These two postcard views amply demonstrate the rapid changes that were taking place along North Broadway in the early years of this century. In card number 196, horse-drawn vehicles still seemed to be the predominant form of transportation along city streets. The view, looking north along Broadway from Grand Avenue, captures the recently completed Lee-Huckins Hotel (card no. 76) on the southeast corner of Main and Broadway. In card number 197, which can be dated some fifteen years later, around 1925, automobiles have entirely displaced the horse. Far from numbering only a few vehicles, as in the previous card, they throng the streets. Already it has become necessary to station a policeman to direct traffic. Much new construction is also in evidence. On the left are the new Tradesmens National Bank (card no. 206) and Medical Arts Building (card no. 46), and on the extreme right is the Herskowitz Building (card no. 43), flying the flags of the United States and the army recruiting office. Oklahoma City was becoming a major metropolis.

196

197

198. Although identified as being "Oklahoma City as seen from an Aeroplane," this appears to be a representation drawn by an artist using an actual photograph as a reference. With the viewpoint looking toward the northeast, the major landmarks are drawn more or less accurately, but the small structures may have been done from imagination. Thought to have been published in the 1920's, the view nicely shows the Oklahoma County Court House with its sidewalks radiating from four sides. North of the Court House lay the Frisco and Rock Island railroad yards, which were moved in another decade and the land they occupied converted to the new Civic Center.

198

Exterior and Interior of S. H. Kress & Co.,
5 and 10c Store, Oklahoma City, Okla.

199. The S. H. Kress & Co. opened for business prior to statehood in the white building (center, bottom photo), and by 1910 had expanded to include both the 217 and 219 West Main addresses as the Kress sign indicates. The Illinois Hotel, with its distinctive arched third-story balcony, was upstairs. Inside, on the ground floor, the Kress Co. was a virtual wonderland of 5¢, 10¢, and 25¢ items that made the firm a nationwide success. The counters were segmented and each space was filled with merchandise that ranged from writing paper and pens to glass candy containers in the shape of a train, world globe, or a rabbit. Former customers recall the wooden floors creaking as they made their way through the aisles.

200. Frederick R. Parsons, the children's portrait artist and proprietor of the Studio Grand, obviously planned for any unexpected emergency, in that he had a fresh banana on hand to occupy the un-cooperative subject of the sitting! In 1907 the Studio Grand was located at 325 North Broadway and became a popular place for parents to bring their children for photographic portraits. Early city directories indicate that Parsons was the only photographer, at least in 1907, with enough grit to "specialize" in children.

201. The expanding economy of Oklahoma City created a need for business college graduates skilled in business techniques. The Capital City Business College at 116 West Second Street was one of several such institutions which students might attend to "learn a paying profession." Instruction was available in the Byrne Simplified Shorthand method, practical bookkeeping, business training, salesmanship, multigraphing, and becoming proficient as a comptometer operator. Furniture in the Capital City Business College was solid oak. Typewriters and other machines were kept in good working order for the six hundred students who trained annually.

200

The Home of Capital City Business College,
Oklahoma City, Okla.

202.   Henry Kamp and his brothers' grocery store has been a fixture at 1314-1316 West Twenty-fifth Street for most of this century. In 1915, as this card proclaims, the business was known as the Epworth View Grocery, the name being taken from Epworth University, a prominent landmark in the area at that time. Today the enterprising brothers who emigrated from Germany and founded one of Oklahoma City's most famous groceries have all passed away, but their store, now known simply as Kamp's, still does business at the same location.

203.   A listing for Westfall's Drug Store first appears in the 1903 city directory, with its location given as 200 West Main, on the southwest corner of Main and Robinson. Its boast of being the largest drugstore in Oklahoma at that time may very well have been legitimate, for it had seven employees, three of whom were registered pharmacists. Later, a branch store was opened at Second and Robinson. Just above its corner entrance was the mortar and pestle trade sign which was to a drugstore what the striped pole was to a barbershop. This view also contains an unexpected feature: note the repairman on top of the telephone pole!

204.   Gentry Cleaners, at 519 North Broadway, was, according to its advertising, "associated with first class cleaning and pressing. Mr. Gentry has been in this city for many years, and his guarantee for first class work is always worth one hundred cents on the dollar. He will send and get your work and deliver all goods promptly. He cleans the most delicate fabrics, and makes a speciality of ladies' work." Gentry also used this postcard, part of a series of twelve, as a premium, giving a different one with each garment left to be cleaned or dyed. When the full set was acquired, the customer was entitled to receive, gratis, a handsome art calendar, from a limited number purchased by Gentry and unobtainable elsewhere!

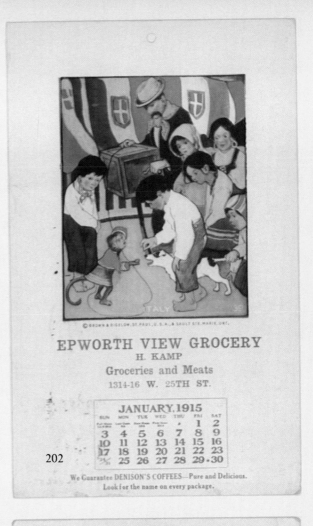

EPWORTH VIEW GROCERY

H. KAMP

Groceries and Meats

1314-16 W. 25TH ST.

JANUARY, 1915

We Guarantee DENISON'S COFFEES—Pure and Delicious.
Look for the name on every package.

202

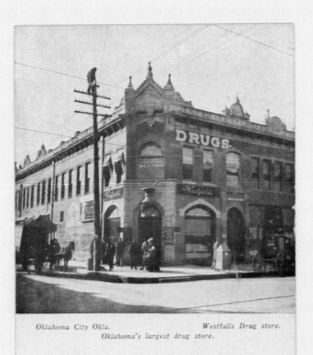

Oklahoma City Okla.   Westfalls Drug store.
Oklahoma's largest drug store.

203

Gentry

FRENCH DRY CLEANING & DYEING

PHONE 606

519
North Broadway
OKLAHOMA
CITY

204

Columbia Bank & Trust Co.
Oklahoma City, Okla.

205

205. The Columbia Bank and Trust Co. at 135 West Main had a grand, bank-like entrance with impressive looking columns on each side of the front door. Alas, the exterior appearance could not influence the decisions that were made inside. Founded in 1905, the bank was forced to close in 1909. Records indicate that it was the first state bank to fail after the adoption of the bank guaranty law; and though the closing prompted a grand jury investigation, the results have never been disclosed. We know only that the bank is supposed to have had a capital of $200,000 in April, 1909, just before it "went under."

206. The Tradesmens National Bank Building, facing south on the northwest corner of Main and Broadway, has long been an imposing structure. It was built in 1923 on the same corner which had been occupied by the grand old Masonic Temple (card no. 91), and later the Western National Bank. The Tradesmens National Bank remained at this location until sometime in 1949, when it was consolidated with the First National Bank, which occupied the taller building on the left edge of this postcard view. Continuing north on Broadway, the four-columned structure is the Security National Bank (card no. 207); the next building, the Egbert Hotel, in which was located the famous Bishop's Restaurant; and then the Medical Arts Building (card no. 46). Note that the streetcar tracks were still evident.

207. The initial home of the Security National Bank appears to have been the "busy corner" that formerly had been the location of the Roach & Veazey Drug Store (card no. 7). By 1915, the bank moved to the stately structure shown in this view. The bank referred to these new quarters as "the finest banking room in Oklahoma, at 109 North Broadway." A decade later the Security National Bank moved again, occupying the entire first floor of the new and impressive Medical Arts Building (card no. 46) on the southwest corner of First (Park) and Broadway.

TRADESMENS NATIONAL BANK BUILDING

Northwest Corner Main and Broadway

OKLAHOMA CITY, OKLAHOMA

206

3A-H624

Security National Bank, Oklahoma City, Okla.

SECURITY NATIONAL BANK

207

208. The details of the history of the Farmers National Bank are well covered by Roy Stewart in his book, **Born Grown.** It was established in 1903 as the Farmers State Bank; then in 1909, after nationalization, became the Farmers National Bank. The decision to build a new home for the bank in 1923, came under the leadership of Dan W. Hogan. The bank acquired temporary quarters in the Colcord Building (card no. 45) while its new home was being constructed on the narrow strip of land east of the Oklahoma Club (card no. 72). This postcard view shows the completed interior of the new bank, adorned with its opening night decorations. Stewart goes on to say: "In 1930 the bank recognized the urbanization of Oklahoma City when it changed its name from Farmers to City National Bank & Trust Company."

209. The Perrine Building, on the southwest corner of Robinson and Park, had the address 119 North Robinson. It was begun in 1926 and completed and opened for occupancy in 1927. It is located immediately west of the First National Bank Building (card no. 210). There has long been a history of extraordinary traffic between the two buildings for business and professional reasons. Later renamed the Cravens Building, many people still associate this name with the structure even though in recent years it has become known as the First Life Assurance Building. Today, the First National Bank owns and manages the building and, as this book goes to press, the future of the old Perrine Building remains uncertain.

210. The photographer stood at a window in the Federal Building to capture this view of two lofty skyscrapers on Robinson Street. The thirty-one story Ramsey Tower, seen on the left, was completed in 1931, and provided office space for those prospering from the oil boom. The building has changed ownership and names numerous times, but is known today as the First City Place Building. The other skyscraper, with the aviation beacon on top, is the First National Bank Building, also completed in 1931.

209

210

211. This full view of the Oklahoma Publishing Company Building probably was taken from the Pioneer Telephone Building (card no. 85) in the spring of 1909. Workmen can be seen installing windows on the two lower floors and doing interior finish work. Built on the northeast corner of Fourth and Broadway, the grandeur of the Layton and Smith design is evident. First occupied on October 10, 1909, the structure is still the home of **The Daily Oklahoman.** In this early image the streetcar tracks turning east from Broadway and going down Fourth Street are easily distinguishable. Notice, too, how a residential section surrounds this new neighbor.

212. W. H. Crump, a native of Illinois, came to Oklahoma City around 1902. His first business venture was the Opera House Drug Store, which he owned and operated. In 1911, he moved to this location at 1400 West Main, adopted the name Crump & Co., and became the local agent for Truax, Green & Co. of Chicago. He carried a complete line of surgical instruments and supplies for physicians and hospitals, and barber supplies of all kinds. Crump & Co. was also a drugstore with a pharmacy, Kodak photo finishing, and, according to the sign on the window, a 5¢ special on cold apple cider. This site was occupied by Crump & Co. until 1921. The building and its occupants have long since faded into history, and today the corner is a vacant lot.

213. This postcard was mailed by a gentleman to a lady admirer in Iowa and the message reads: "Snap shot of a few of us just before lunch. We would have looked more pleasant after eating. [signed] Charlie." This 8 North Broadway location for the Wells Fargo & Company Express office is easily placed in perspective by referring to the view of the Campbell Building (card no. 44) next door to the north. Another local facility of this famous express company is on card no. 114, which shows the Wells Fargo livery stable across from the Missouri, Kansas & Texas Railroad depot on East Reno.

214. In this interesting photographic postcard three gentlemen pose confidently with this 1910 vintage open automobile in front of the Townsend-Curreathers Hat Company at 204-206 West Second Street. Next door, behind a plate glass window, a fourth man stands by a dressmaker's model, looking out on the scene with a somewhat disgusted expression. It is only speculation, but the three men with the car could be the officers of the T.-C. Hat Co.: J. H. Townsend, president; J. D. Curreathers, vice-president; and R. L. Knight, secretary-treasurer. Or, they may just be "dudes" out test-driving one of the sports models from "automobile alley" on North Broadway.

215. This view shows the northwest corner of Northeast Second and Stiles, the location of the Slaughter Building, also, in its heyday, known as Doctors' Row. Around 1903, Dr. Wyatt H. Slaughter came to Oklahoma City and is said to have been the first black physician to establish a medical practice here. Other physicians also set up offices in this building, and a drug store was opened on the corner. Upstairs was a small auditorium and dances were sometimes held in the building. Dr. Slaughter was a respected leader in the black community and assumed an active role in working for equal opportunities in the late 1930's. The old Slaughter Building is still standing.

216. In 1910, the National Builders Supply Company officed in the Campbell Building (card no. 44), with Arthur M. Lutes as president and George C. Gray as treasurer. The city directory of the same year noted that the firm manufactured gas-burned building brick and that it stocked all kinds of high-grade building materials. By 1911 the company occupied this interesting structure at 619 West Main. The carved eagle standing on a shield just below the American flag emphasized the "national" in its name, a trade mark the management no doubt hoped would remind prospective customers to "buy American" at the National Builders Supply Company. Records are scarce, but it is believed that this building was gone prior to 1920.

The best lighted and ventilated Laundry
in the South West,
Broadway Circle, Oklahoma City, Okla.

217. Where speed and promptness would normally have seemed the best virtues to promote, the Dinks Parrish's Slowest Laundry Company at 2 Broadway Circle adopted a different approach and became quite successful. Dinks specialized in laundering fine linen and in being slow and careful. It had a repair department where buttons were replaced, socks darned, and new collar bands put on shirts. All repairs were neatly done. Also, Dinks provided private suitcases to carry linens to the residences of its customers. Ladies' skirts and gowns were packed in cartons, the same length as the garments, to insure their safe delivery.

Furrow & Company, Oklahoma City, Okla.

218. From the message side of this postcard we know that this picture was taken during the Easter season of 1916. An abundance of traditional potted plants was available for the walk-in trade. The cooler in the rear of the store held cut flowers for special arrangements. Furrow & Company had a good downtown location, 120 West Main, with considerable pedestrian traffic passing by its front windows every day. The 1917 city directory listed Lon Foster as the manager, and the 1920 edition indicated that the business had moved to 122 North Robinson, with the name changed to Foster Floral Company. Lon Foster was making his mark in his chosen profession!

Foster Floral Co.
First and Robinson
Oklahoma City

219. Lon Foster, Sr., of the Foster Floral Company at First and Robinson, said in the June 17, 1928 issue of **The Daily Oklahoman,** "I believe that anything that can be grown anywhere can be grown in Oklahoma City." He went on to prove his point by becoming the only orchid-growing florist this side of Los Angeles. Later, in 1937, the Foster Floral advertising boasted of having more refrigerated display space than any other flower shop in the United States. This display was backed by the company's seven huge steel-framed modern greenhouses and seventeen acres of land stocked with exquisite growing flowers! Now in its third generation within the same family, the business is known as Foster Flowers & Gifts and is located at 1520 Northwest Twenty-third Street.

220. The John Deere Plow Company Building at 531-539 West Main, directly north of the County Court House, was first occupied by this famous farm implement firm sometime in 1907. The company's trademark deer is silhouetted against the sky at the top-center of the front facade. By the late 1920's, the O. K. Transfer and Storage Company had taken over the structure and the John Deere Plow Company had moved to a new location in the warehouse district. The building shown here was demolished sometime in the 1960's, replaced by the parking lot which now occupies this site. John Deere was one of several major farm implement companies which sold many carloads of machinery to farmers and ranchers in the early days of Oklahoma City.

221. "You can drink Ozarka Spring Water in your home or office for a few cents a week. Give Ozarka Spring Water a month's trial and see the wonderful improvement in your health." The Ozarka Water Company shipped this water in glass lined tank cars from Eureka Springs, Arkansas to its bottling plant in Oklahoma City. Here it was stored and delivered in five gallon glass bottles. Six delivery trucks served customers at the time this colorful advertising postcard was distributed, sometime in the mid-1930's. The firm continues to do business at its present location, 729 Southwest Third Street.

222. This is an example of a postcard used by a salesman who would soon be calling on a potential customer. The message reads: "Will call for an order for Loose-Wiles products on 7/14/09. Wait for me. Sincerely, Herbert, salesman." Loose-Wiles had an extensive operation in Oklahoma City from the time of statehood through most of World War II. The company is remembered for a variety of tasty cracker and biscuit products. This rare view shows the mixing room in the cracker department.

30 Views in Loose-Wiles Factory—No. 3.   Section of Mixing Room---Cracker Dept.

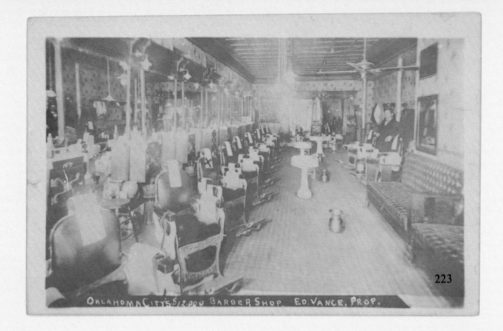

Oklahoma City's $12000 Barber Shop. Ed. Vance, Prop.

223. Ed Vance was the proprietor of this swell barbershop in downtown Oklahoma City, circa 1909. The postcard title indicates that it cost $12,000, and while this seems substantial, this was a big operation, able to serve quite a clientele! Thirteen chairs were poised for customers and porcelain sinks and brass spitoons were strategically positioned. The tufted leather benches inside the entrance offered gentlemen a place to wait for their choice of barber. A great rack in the back of the shop held the personal shaving mugs of regular customers. Big deals were being made all over town and a man wanted to look his best!

224. The MacArthur Photo Service was owned and managed by Fred MacArthur, a prominent early-day photographer and civic leader. Prior to his arrival in Oklahoma City in 1914, he had worked as a cowboy in the Glass Mountains region of northwestern Oklahoma. This early photo postcard shows his shop on the northwest corner of Linwood and Klein. In the mid-1930's the MacArthur firm was developing and printing between 3,000 and 5,000 Kodak pictures per day for local camera owners. A number of the real photographic postcards in this study have the MacArthur name on the edge of the message side, indicating that he was making a number of prints into postcards. The firm no longer exists, but the remodeled building still stands.

Patterson Bldg., Oklahoma City.

225. The narrow part of the Patterson Building faced north on Main while the longer side faced east toward the streetcar terminal between Harvey and Hudson. Without a doubt, the Patterson Building, erected in 1910, was the most ornately decorated structure in the city. There was an incredible display of terra cotta work on the exterior as shown in this view. In her study on architect Solomon Layton, who designed the Patterson, Mary Jo Nelson stated: "The crowning feature was twelve cast-iron baroque lighting fixtures spaced along the top cornice. Each one held a huge opaque lead glass light globe." The Patterson was eventually renamed the Equity Building and still later it was incorporated into the Kerr's Department Store complex, of which only photographic memories remain.

226. Has no one heard about banker's hours? The Night and Day Bank at 33 West Main opened its doors for business on March 11, 1909. Its advertising bombshell was that it opened Monday through Friday at 8 o'clock in the morning and remained open until 8 o'clock in the evening. Saturday hours were 8 o'clock to 10 o'clock in the evening. Can you imagine such banking hours! The Night and Day Bank lasted until sometime in 1911 when it merged with the Wilkin-Hale State Bank, an institution which failed in 1922. Buster Brown, his dog Tige, and Buster's sweetheart Mary Jane were all smiles in this advertising postcard mailed in February, 1910 to potential customers.

227. George Barnett's Cigar Store, on City Hall Corner at Grand and Broadway, was a classy place! Just feast your eyes on the octagonal showcase, sitting on its marble base and filled with meerschaum pipes, and there on top is a water pipe! Brass cuspidors, handy for men who found it necessary to expectorate, were among the items offered for sale. The mural and the coffered ceiling accented the cases which were filled with tobaccos and cigars, and, as the postcard suggests, "smokers novelties." The cigar was the social after-dinner pleasure that many men would take from their pockets, ignite with great ceremony, and make a showy production of savoring. The woods were full of different kinds of cigars and chewing tobaccos, and almost every community had at least two or three of its own local brands and plugs. Situated so near City Hall, there just had to have been lots of whoppers told at Barnett's.

228. Established in October, 1899, and incorporated two months later, the Alexander Drug Company (card no. 22) celebrated its twenty-eighth anniversary by purchasing an entire section of **The Daily Oklahoman** on Sunday, June 24, 1928. Here the copy told of a room filled with hundreds of cases with "one of everything" displayed, but nothing sold: this was the sample room. Everything was represented from bathing caps to fountain pens. To quote: "'Try the drug store first,' said the wag, 'and if it isn't there it ain't.'" Testimonials included one from an army officer's wife stationed in Puerto Rico who was faced with an ant problem. She wrote to Alexander's and received an "ant lacquer" for the extermination of the pests. Later her friends ordered huge quantities of "Ant Bate."

RESOLVED THAT THE BANK THAT STRIKES MY HEART IS THE ONE THAT IS GLAD TO ACCOMMODATE IT'S PATRONS EVERY DAY AND NIGHT IN THE YEAR. BUSTER BROWN.

WHY NOT DO BUSINESS WITH THE BEST BANK—THE *Night and Day Bank* OKLAHOMA CITY OKLAHOMA

Interest paid on Time Deposits and Savings Accounts
ABNER DAVIS, President   F. H. MYERS, Cashier

227

228

OKLAHOMA COUNTY COURT HOUSE, OKLAHOMA CITY, OKLA.

229

229. Completed in 1936 as a Public Works Administration project, the Oklahoma County Court House at 321 Park Avenue is on the eastern boundary of the Civic Center complex. Having long since outgrown the former Court House shown on the cover of the first volume of **The Vanished Splendor,** the county commissioned the design of this new structure from the firm of Layton and Forsyth. It was built for $1,200,000 with the expectation that it would provide the needed office space for county government for many years to come. These best intentions were frustrated and, once again, numerous agencies are housed elsewhere throughout the county.

Civic Center by Night, Oklahoma City, Okla.

230

230. The Civic Center, shown here in an unusual nighttime postcard view, was partially financed by Public Works grants during the Depression and was built on land formerly occupied by railroad tracks. The Frisco and Rock Island lines had run through mid-Oklahoma City, but when these lines began to be serviced by the new Union Station (card no. 112), the right-of-way in the center of town became available and was the location for the new Oklahoma County Court House, the Municipal Building, and the Municipal Auditorium. In his book **Born Grown,** Roy Stewart gives much of the credit for the realization of this civic center concept to the city manager, Orval "Red" Mosier.

231. Oklahoma City, with its many hotels, Coliseums (cards no. 123 and 311), and City Auditorium (card no. 177) suitable for large gatherings, has long been a convention center. The community was made even more attractive to convention planners with the construction of the Municipal Auditorium. Designed by architect J. O. Parr and built and equipped at a cost in excess of $1,260,000 in the mid-1930's, this grand structure has served countless thousands of out-of-town guests as well as the local citizenry. The main auditorium seated over 7,000 people, while another 4,000 could be easily accommodated in the basement for meetings or trade shows. It also featured committee rooms, conference areas, and a Little Theatre. After extensive renovation several years ago, the Municipal Auditorium was renamed the Civic Center Music Hall.

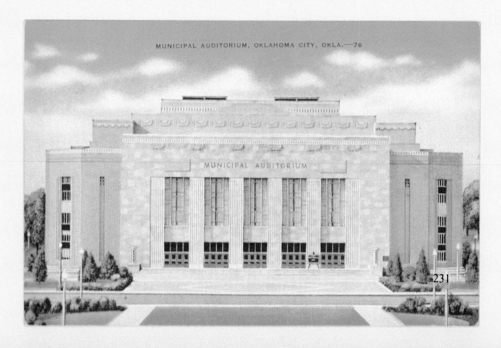

MUNICIPAL AUDITORIUM, OKLAHOMA CITY, OKLA.—76

MUNICIPAL AUDITORIUM

231

232. The Municipal Building, also known as City Hall, was part of the overall Civic Center development. Built at 200 North Walker with its main entrance facing west, the east side, shown here, looked to a reflecting basin and illuminated fountain. The Municipal Building, erected at a cost of $600,000, was designed by an eleven member group known as the Allied Architects. It is the core location of much of Oklahoma City's government, housing the mayor, city manager, city clerk, city treasurer, city attorney, and numerous city-related services. As Oklahoma City has grown, so has the need for the many public agencies that handle services from building permits to animal control. Presently, however, many of these agencies have outgrown their original quarters in City Hall and have been forced to seek office space nearby.

City Hall, Oklahoma City, Oklahoma — D-1

233. Notice the arched openings on top of the tower on the Federal Court House Building and then look back at the arched frame on postcard view no. 210 showing the two lofty skyscrapers, and you will see that this was indeed the photographer's vantage point. The location of the Federal Building is the entire block along Northwest Third, from Robinson to Harvey. The former Post Office (card no. 40) can be seen on the right end of this structure and its mate, which was mentioned in the earlier description, is on the far left or west end. Dating back to territorial days, Saint Joseph's Cathedral (card no. 26) is easily spotted in the upper left corner. Notice also the many residences and apartment buildings along Fourth Street and further north.

POST OFFICE AND GOVERNMENT BLDG., OKLAHOMA CITY, OKLA.—34

234. This view looks south on Lincoln Boulevard, toward the north face of the Oklahoma State Capitol. Northeast Twenty-third Street runs east and west. In this 1920's scene there is a filling station on each corner, and both Twenty-third Street and Lincoln are two-lane streets. Today, each is a six-lane thoroughfare. Two state office buildings, the Will Rogers Building and Sequoyah Building, are now situated on these same corners; the shade trees were removed years ago. In sixty years the atmosphere of the area has changed markedly. Only the Capitol Building itself remains un-altered from its original state. Incidentally, the north face of the Capitol is considered the rear entrance.

OKLAHOMA STATE CAPITOL from Lincoln Blvd.

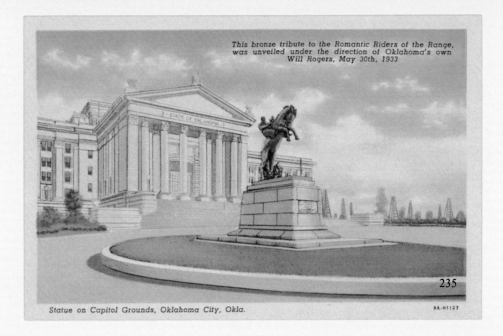

This bronze tribute to the Romantic Riders of the Range, was unveiled under the direction of Oklahoma's own Will Rogers, May 30th, 1933

235

Statue on Capitol Grounds, Oklahoma City, Okla.

9A-H1127

235. Madame Constance Whitney Warren, an American artist living in Paris, France arranged through her father to give Oklahoma her original sculptured work, "Cowboy on a Wild Pony." Some shenanigans must have occurred, because the location for the statue was not as stipulated by the senate resolution, but instead, the statue was placed in front of the south entrance of the Capitol. Furthermore, this postcard, and the statue's bronze plaque erroneously indicate that Will Rogers was present at the dedication. However, he was unable to attend and the statue remained covered with a tarpaulin for several months. The sculpture was not officially dedicated until twenty-seven years later by Governor Raymond Gary on November 14, 1957.

State of Oklahoma Capitol Office Building, Capitol Grounds, Oklahoma City, Okla.

236

3B-H272

236. Twenty-one years after the State Capitol was built, the Capitol Office Building, shown here in this view, was completed in November, 1938 at a cost of $800,000. Originally, it was to house these expanding state departments: the highway commission, tax commission, Oklahoma public welfare commission, and the safety commission. Later renamed the Jim Thorpe Building, after the state's famous Indian athlete, the building has become part of the maze of office buildings, on all sides of the State Capitol, which provide for the seemingly unending expansion of state government services.

GOVERNOR'S MANSION AND STATE OWNED WELLS IN OKLAHOMA CITY, OKLAHOMA

237

6A-H1394

237. Completed in 1928 at a cost of $75,000, this nineteen-room Dutch Colonial mansion has been the home of fourteen different governors and their families. William Judson Holloway was its first occupant, followed by the controversial William H. "Alfalfa Bill" Murray, who uprooted the lawn and plowed the earth with mules so that it might be planted with vegetables for needy Oklahomans. Later the mansion was re-landscaped, and further improvements have been made through the years when needed. The home is located two blocks east of the Capitol and faces west. Self-guided tours are permitted at specified times and guests are encouraged to tour the home that is the official state residence.

238. Sometime in 1938 the Borden Company bought the Evans Milk Company and its facilities at 2126 North Broadway. The building shown in this postcard was constructed at a cost of $250,000 and had its official opening on May 15, 1947. The Chamber of Commerce board of directors was invited for a tour and **The Daily Oklahoman** reported that instead of the fifteen or twenty that were expected, a crowd of seventy-five bankers, preachers, businessmen, and industrialists showed up for the tour and the free strawberry sundaes afterwards. The Borden Company continues to provide the community with its quality products.

239. The "W & W" initials in the name W & W Steel Company stand for W. G. Wilson and John H. Winneberger. These two men joined forces in the immediate post-World War II era and founded their business on October 1, 1945. Their base of operations was, and continues to be, 1730 West Reno in Oklahoma City. The company specializes in the fabrication of reinforcing steel, structural steel, and ornamental iron. In an earlier day its advertising declared, "Everything STEEL for Buildings." The business has expanded over the years and today includes a plant in Norman, Oklahoma and facilities in Albuquerque, New Mexico and Lubbock, Texas.

240. Otto E. Hart, a "self-made man," immigrated to this country from Austria and found work wherever it was available. He arrived in Oklahoma City in 1921 and worked for a cousin who owned a candy store. By attending night school, he learned the language of his adopted country. Hart followed the oil boom to Borger, Texas, moving there in 1926 and opening a welding supply firm. Returning to Oklahoma City in 1932, he founded the Hart Welding Supply Company, located first at 411 West California, and then, after 1948, at 726 West Grand as shown in this postcard. Today the Hart Industrial Supply Company is a subsidiary of L.S.B. Industries and is one of the largest concerns of its type in the area. Otto Hart passed away in 1963.

MID-CONTINENT LIFE INSURANCE CO. — OKLAHOMA CITY, OKLA.

241. The Mid-Continent Life Insurance Company's home office is located at 1400 Classen Drive. The headquarters, now beautifully landscaped, was officially dedicated in May, 1927. J. H. Frederickson and Company, contractors, built this structure, which is 150 feet long by 70 feet wide and four stories high. The total floor space is 42,000 square feet. Local and regional suppliers were used for nearly all the materials needed in construction. The main entrance doors and electrical fixtures are bronze, as is the hardware used throughout, including the specially cast bronze door knobs bearing the company's insignia. The exposed woodwork in the building is mahogany imported from British Honduras.

HOME STATE LIFE INSURANCE COMPANY BUILDING and THEATER Sixth and Robinson OKLAHOMA CITY, OKLA.

242. Initially this imposing building was known as the India Temple Shrine and was built in 1923 for over a million dollars. The local Masonic lodges united to construct a meeting place where they might all assemble. The impressive results were designed by Layton, Forsyth, and Hicks. During the Depression years, title was lost by the Masons and the building was eventually sold at auction. In the late 1940's it became the headquarters of the Home State Life Insurance Company and the Home Theatre, as depicted in this view. Presently the structure is known as the Journal Record Building and is the home of **The Journal Record.** Incidentally, the movie advertised on the marquee in this view is **The Corpse Came C.O.D.,** starring George Brent and Joan Blondell.

18th and WESTERN
PHONE 4-2276

14th and ROBINSON
PHONE 7-1422

Peacock Cleaners

243. Peacock Cleaners, "where the charm of newness is restored," first opened at 1018 Northwest Eighteenth Street in the late 1930's and remained there until the early 1950's. A second location was established in early 1940, at 1428 North Robinson. By 1958 both stores had discontinued business. A stuffed peacock, perched near the register at both locations, tacitly emphasized the old saying, "proud as a peacock." What better slogan could possibly be used for such a business! Peacock chose, however, to become recognized as the "wear clean clothes" cleaners.

244. C. E. Keeton headed the Keeton Ice Company located at 1501 Southwest Twenty-ninth Street. By 1937, his operation at this address had expanded to include the Keeton Filling Station, which sold Phillips 66 gasoline, oil, tires, batteries, radios, and accessories, as well as ice. At this time the business claimed to have twenty-two employees. This real photograph postcard was mailed in 1935 to a potential customer in Capitol Hill, perhaps to advise the addressee of the service that was available. The delivery truck is parked in front, ready to roll.

244

Keeton Ice Co.
1501 S.W 29th.
3-8922.

245. The Morgan Building, with oil derrick behind, still stands today much as it did in the late 1940's when this photograph was taken at the southeast corner of Fourth and Durland. At that time, it was the home of Dr. C. Wesley Morgan's well-equipped, fourteen-room office. It also housed the ultra-modern dental office of Dr. Byron Biscoe. Other occupants of the building included Dr. Dewey Moore's Prescription Shop, on the ground level corner; Black's popular flower shop, owned by Mr. and Mrs. Charles Pollard; Thelma's House of Beauty, complete with the latest equipment, owned by Mrs. T. Johnson; and the reliable East-Side Radio and Electric Shop, owned by Mr. James Johnson. On the lower floor was the swanky and comfortable lounge of the Kappa Alpha Psi Fraternity.

245

246. With WKY (card no. 63) as the first in the city, a second radio station, carrying the call letters KFJF, came to Oklahoma City in March, 1926. A 1927 program schedule lists "Special Features" for Friday evening listening as the Fidelity String Quartet from 8:00 to 9:30, and a Klan talk by the Grand Dragon of the Realm of Oklahoma from 9:30 to 10:00. On Saturday night, from 10:00 to 1:00, was the American Legion Weekly Radio Frolic. The studio view shown here, with the KFJF microphone in the foreground, and others placed around the room, indicates that many of the musical programs originated from this room. By October, 1932, KFJF had become KOMA, was affiliated with the Columbia Broadcasting Company, and had moved its studios to the Biltmore (card no. 287).

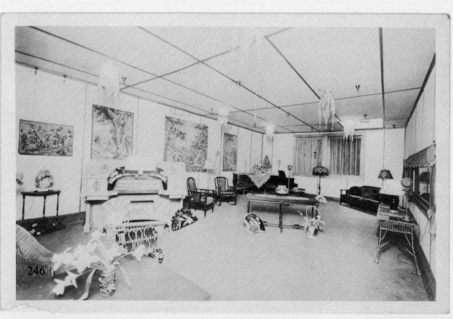

246

SOUTHWEST BELL TELEPHONE BUILDING, OKLAHOMA CITY, OKLA.

247

247. The Pioneer Telephone Building (card no. 85) is nearly dwarfed by the sixteen-story buff-colored brick building on its north side. This larger structure is the Southwestern Bell Telephone Building which was constructed in 1927, with occupancy beginning in 1928. General acceptance of the telephone and its growing use in the Oklahoma City area forced the construction of this larger building in order to handle additional equipment, offices, and new systems. About this time there was a transition away from operator assistance for each call to the direct dial system. Fireproof construction was used throughout the building and a supplemental power plant was designed to provide continuous telephone service in case of emergency.

248. It is hard to imagine today that Oklahoma City was once so far in the distance from the WKY Radio transmitter, located on East Britton Road. At the time this postcard was published, WKY boasted of being a part of the NBC Network, and having studios in the Skirvin Tower Hotel. But it was the tallest of the three towers shown here that generated the most pride, for this was a new $250,000 transmitter, 915 feet high, twice as tall as Oklahoma City's highest skyscraper and, at the time, the sixth tallest man-made structure in the western hemisphere. WKY had every reason to be proud.

249. This stately "Tower of Memories" was dedicated to the members of the American Legion. A plaque on the tower reads: "Cornerstone laid November 11, 1928 by members of American Legion Post 35." The tower was completed in 1929, and is located in Memorial Park Cemetery, "The Garden of Memories," on North Kelley and Memorial Road. In recent years a sound system has been installed which plays recorded chimes and bells during services.

NEW TRANSMITTER
RADIO STATION WKY
OKLAHOMA CITY

248

249

THE CHIMES TOWER — "MEMORIAL PARK CEMETERY"

250. Initially the business on the northwest corner of Northwest Twelfth and Robinson was known as the "Home Undertakers-Watts and McAtee." By the mid-1940's, the business was renamed simply the Watts Funeral Home. It operated from this beautiful three-story structure which was expanded several times in later years. In 1967 the Watts Funeral Home moved to a new location in the northwest part of town, only to cease operations a few years later. The structure at the former location was razed and today the corner is a vacant lot.

250
WATTS FUNERAL HOME
OKLAHOMA CITY

251. The Ben. V. Hunter Funeral Home at 2427 South Harvey has served the southern part of Oklahoma City for nearly half a century. In the spring of 1938 it announced an open house and dedication of the facility shown in this postcard view. The memory chapel has a beautiful pipe organ and offers families a stately, church-like atmosphere in their time of need.

251

THE BEN V. HUNTER FUNERAL HOME — OKLAHOMA CITY

252. In 1924, this beautiful mausoleum, built at a cost of $144,920, was constructed in the Fairlawn Cemetery at 2700 North Shartel. It contains individual and family crypts. There are numerous stained glass windows, including a special one entitled, "The Flight of the Soul," signed by the artist, Louis Comfort Tiffany. Fairlawn Cemetery was incorporated in 1892 and is known as Oklahoma City's pioneer cemetery. Every lot owner becomes a stockholder in a mutual corporation and the profits are invested in perpetual care.

BEAUTIFUL NEW MAUSOLEUM - In Fairlawn Cemetery
Oklahoma City's Pioneer Cemetery
ENID K. WEISS, Secretary

252

OKLAHOMA'S LARGEST FORD DEALER

253. Fred Jones opened his Fred Jones Motor Company at 220 West Reno on September 1, 1922. The business prospered and fifteen years later, on December 30, 1937, he invited the public to attend the formal opening of his new showroom at 200 South Harvey, as shown in this postcard view. By this time, with an annual payroll of over $200,000, he employed 125 people and had become one of the four largest Ford, Lincoln and Lincoln-Zephyr dealers in the United States. A complete line of the new 1938 Ford V-8's was shown that opening night and fresh cut flowers, delivered by airplane from Mexico City, were presented to the ladies as favors.

"Southwest's Greatest Automotive Institution"

254. Walter E. Allen moved from Detroit to Oklahoma City in early 1940 after purchasing the Chrysler and Plymouth distributorship for central and western Oklahoma. Initially the salesroom was at 1117 North Robinson, but from 1946 through 1955 its location was at Thirteenth and Harvey. Carl P. Smith was Walter Allen's top salesman and was featured on this advertising postcard in 1953. Carl obviously enjoyed his position because when his third son was born, the child was named Walter Allen Smith in honor of the car dealer. Employees still fondly recall the annual Christmas party with its elaborate buffet dinner, and Carl playing Santa Claus. Although Mr. Allen retired in 1955 and moved to Florida, Carl Smith continued selling automobiles, this time for the local Cadillac dealership.

255. The Kinnebrew Motor Company operated first from an 800 North Broadway address, and then in 1937 moved to this 701 North Broadway location on the northwest corner of Sixth and Broadway. From the time when some of the earliest automobile dealerships were established here, Broadway became fondly known as "automobile alley," with an entire range of makes and models being offered up and down both sides of the street. During this period Oklahoma City was experiencing tremendous growth and the automobile as a status symbol was not overlooked! Traditionally, the first floors of these motor car buildings were used as showrooms, and the upper levels for parts and repair work. The Nash, Lafayette, and Pierce-Arrow were all sold at Kinnebrew's. The C. R. Anthony corporate headquarters occupies this site today.

256. Robert McDonald opened his Chevrolet automobile business in 1932. Then, in the early 1940's, R. Thornton Scott joined the business, forming the partnership of McDonald-Scott Chevrolet Company. Its office, showroom, and garage facilities, shown in this view, were located at the corner of Seventh and Broadway. During the war years, when automobile plants were converted to war use, the car dealers only had service and used cars to market. In 1957 the firm became Scott Chevrolet and expanded to occupy the better part of three blocks between Seventh and Tenth Streets on North Broadway. In 1980 Steve Burke Chevrolet bought out the Scott dealership, but recently closed its doors. Currently, developer J. D. Lobb is renovating a number of buildings in the area for his planned Broadway Reunion Center.

McDONALD-SCOTT CHEVROLET COMPANY OKLAHOMA CITY OKLAHOMA 256

257. The message on this postcard reads: "Dear Friend — I've just seen the '49 Plymouth - Wow! ... They sure saved the best for the last! Fretwell Motor Co. will have it on display Mar. 18th till 10 p.m. Be sure to go by and have a look, you'll agree with me, its out of this world!" The Fretwell Motor Company was located on the southeast corner of Fourth and Shartel and was first listed at this location in the 1938 city directory. The firm had been doing business elsewhere in the city for fourteen years prior to this. It sold Plymouth and De Soto automobiles. Sooner Chrysler Plymouth Inc. took over the location in the early 1970's, but by 1983 the building was razed and the land today is part of the Sycamore Square condominium development.

257 FRETWELL MOTOR CO. OKLAHOMA CITY

258. The postage on this postcard was 2¢ in 1956 when Sears mailed it to a customer urging her to come to the curtain and bedspread department. So many changes! On March 15, 1954 the old Sears Roebuck and Co. store at Grand and Harvey closed and on March 25th the new store was officially opened at 2101 Northwest Twenty-third, on the northwest corner of Twenty-third and Pennsylvania. The location had formerly been part of the G. T. Shepherd family's homestead. Sears offered so much for their customers: complete air conditioning, smooth escalators, a spacious snack bar, cosmetics and drugs, a complete garden shop, a super service station, and free parking for 750 cars.

SEARS, ROEBUCK AND CO. — OKLAHOMA CITY'S MOST MODERN DEPARTMENT STORE

ALWAYS PLENTY OF FREE PARKING AT N. W. 23rd AND PENN., IN SEARS BIG LIGHTED AND PAVED PARKING LOT — NOW ROOM FOR 1,200 CARS
258

259

259. The University Station, located on Classen Boulevard near its intersection with Seventeenth Street, was an important facility of the Oklahoma Railway Company. Here, at the junction of two streetcar lines, one could board the El Reno or Guthrie interurbans — which ran on an hourly basis seven days a week — or catch a local car to reach some point within the city. The viewpoint of this card is looking west across Classen toward Epworth University, whose building can just be seen behind the station's tiled roof on the right. When streetcar service was discontinued in 1947, University Station was demolished, and today nothing remains to mark its site but a small, triangular traffic island at Seventeenth and Classen.

FIRST BATTLESHIP BUILT IN OKLAHOMA.
LAUNCHED JULY 4TH '07, BY GRAND RAPIDS FURNITURE CO.

260

260. The Grand Rapids Furniture Company, located at 214-216 West Main, produced this combination patriotic and advertising postcard and probably gave them away to customers during the summer of 1907. The firm offered a full line of roll-top desks, flat top desks, standing desks, revolving chairs and stools, sectional book cases, filing cabinets ... so many items in fact that the management felt you would find whatever you wanted without looking further. Out-of-town customers were courted with chauffeured automobiles and the pledge to pay freight charges on all orders of $5.00 or more. The company literature stated: "Our windows boast of the largest plate glass in Oklahoma, and the building is furnished with passenger and freight elevators."

261. This captured two-man Japanese submarine was in Oklahoma City in November, 1943, as part of a nationwide drive, by the Treasury Department, to sell war bonds and stamps. The eighty-one foot submarine had sixty windows cut into the sides for people to see where "two dummies in Jap uniforms" appeared to be manning the craft. Following a successful tour in Enid and Guthrie, the submarine, preceded by the Naval Air Station Band from Norman, was paraded downtown along North Broadway. Thousands of people purchased war stamps (the minimum being 25¢ for a child, $1.00 for an adult) in order to tour the submarine. Disabled veteran Palmer W. Foley collected a picture of the event and published this postcard after the war as part of a historical series.

U. S. AT WAR WITH JAPAN
December 8, 1941

REMEMBER PEARL HARBOR

I am a disabled overseas veteran and my hobby is collecting pictures and taking pictures with historical background.

PALMER W. FOLEY

261

262. This view is of the "House of Defense" which was built in the Civic Center, west of Walker Avenue, and formally dedicated on December 4, 1941. The cost of this modernistic glass brick structure and the salary of the personnel on duty was borne by the Phillips Petroleum Company as part of its support of the defense savings campaign. There was a belfry housing a fire bell which was rung each time a $25 defense bond sale was made. **The Daily Oklahoman** reported that no bonds were actually sold at the booth, but anyone expressing a desire to make a purchase was transported in an Army jeep to the nearest office where bond sales were made.

263. The United Service Organization, better known as the U.S.O., was located at 431 West Main. Its operation was assisted with staffing and administration by the local YMCA and YWCA. The Jewish Welfare Board was also affiliated with this organization by June, 1944. The U.S.O. Club was a serviceman's headquarters, offering conveniences and diversions such as correspondence desks, laundry facilities, big comfortable divans, overnight bunks, a library, chess and checkers, ping-pong, archery, and a cookie jar ... a real home away from home.

264. $6,500 was contributed locally during a United Service Organization drive in 1942, and this was combined with $7,000 of Public Works Administration funds for a new soldiers' recreation center in downtown Oklahoma City. Located at 208 North Broadway, next to the public comfort station north of the Skirvin Hotel, it was designed to serve the recreation needs of servicemen away from their posts.
Somewhere along the way the Salvation Army must have had a hand in the administration of the club, for telephone books from June, 1943, through December, 1945, list it as the "U.S.O. Club Salvation Army." The site is now occupied by the Skirvin Hotel Motor Lobby.

265

265. The horse-drawn fire-fighting equipment featured in this real photo view is a spring-loaded, sixty-five foot aerial wooden ladder truck. The building in the background, located on the northwest corner of Broadway and California, was the Central Fire Station. Mark Kessler, Fire Chief during the era of this photograph (1903-1919), came to the city fathers' attention when he was Chief of the Guthrie Fire Department. He arrived on a special train with his men to fight a major blaze at the Lion Store which threatened to engulf the entire city. Fire units also came from as far away as El Reno and Purcell, and together they brought the fire under control.

266

266. This real photo view taken in front of the No. 3 Fire Station at 1111 North Hudson, looks to the northwest. The three homes in the background, facing south onto West Park, still stand today, although all have undergone extensive remodeling. The man holding the reins in the buggy has been identified as A. G. "Tony" Myers, who joined the Oklahoma City Fire Department on February 4, 1900. On October 16, 1904, he was appointed Assistant Fire Chief; and from 1919 to 1921, he served as Fire Chief. The No. 3 Fire Station, built in 1905, was a two-story red brick building with two large front doors. This building was razed in the 1930's and replaced with a one-story structure which is no longer used as a fire station.

267

Office, Factory and Warehouse, Oklahoma City, Okla.

267. The offices, salesrooms, storerooms, and yards of the Curtis and Gartside Company were located at 701-715 West Main Street. Established in territorial days, C. S. Curtis served as its president and A. L. Gartside as secretary. A three-story brick building, measuring eighty by one hundred and seventy feet, and equipped with facilities for the receipt, handling, and shipment of the concern's large and varied stock, served as the company's headquarters. It offered sashes, doors, and glass, with specialties in glazed windows, mouldings, interior finishing products, blocks, porch columns, newels, balusters, spindles, brackets, front doors, screen doors, putty, building paper, ruberoid roofing, window glass, fancy glass, and skylight glass. These folks had it all!

268. The name of this apartment house, misspelled in the title, should read "Juprenka" Apartments, a name that was formed by combining the first syllables of the given names of three members of the builder's family: Judy, Prentiss, and Kathryn Price. The October 16, 1916 edition of **The Daily Oklahoman** told of the $60,000 apartment house which would offer occupants "the pleasure of no investment in household goods, for it is the aim of the management to furnish everything, including linen, silver, china, glassware, and even dish towels. The basement will be fitted into an amusement parlor with billiard tables, a victrola and card tables, for the diversion of guests." Today the Juprenka has been renamed the "1321 Harvey Apartments" after its street address. The small wooden structure in front, called a "pergola," was removed around 1950.

269. Dr. Alfred R. Spriggs, an Oklahoma City physician, was the founder and proprietor of the Spriggs Flats, or Spriggs Hotel, at 801-803 Northwest Ninth. He and his wife Marie lived in the hotel, managing it from 1910 until after World War II. In 1961 the building was thoroughly remodeled and the front porches with their Ionic columns were removed. At this time it became the St. Ann Apartments, the name by which it is known to this day. The Spriggs "hotel" was typical of hundreds of smaller apartment houses which are found throughout the older section of Oklahoma City. This view is probably an early one considering the meager number of trees and the temporary fence which undoubtedly protected a new lawn.

270. Located at 112 Northwest Seventh, the Martinique Hotel opened its doors sometime in 1911. Its name was apparently derived from one Henry Martin, an early-day proprietor. In the 1940's, when this attractive postcard was published, the Martinique was owned and managed by a husband and wife team, Mr. and Mrs. Paul V. Funk. In 1960 the Martinique was sold to Maxwell Kaufman, who changed its name to the Maxwell House Apartments, the name which it bears to this day. Having lately passed through a succession of owners and undergone extensive renovation, the complex at present contains thirty-three units and caters primarily to retirees.

J. M. REMINGTON DRUG CO., OKLAHOMA CITY, OKLA.
LEE-HUCKINS HOTEL BUILDING.

271

J. M. REMINGTON DRUG CO., OKLAHOMA CITY, OKLA.
LEE-HUCKINS HOTEL BUILDING.

HAND-COLORED

272

LADIES' RECEPTION PARLOR, LEE-HUCKINS HOTEL,
OKLAHOMA CITY, OKLA.

273

271, 272.   Commercial properties fronting on the corner of Main and Broadway were offered when the new fireproof Lee-Huckins Hotel opened for business in the early part of 1910. One of these prime locations became the home of the J. M. Remington Drug Company, which remained there for several years.

A close examination of the interior views shown on these two postcards will perhaps sharpen the senses of the reader who might remember the unique smells that came from the pharmacy area. The pharmacist was usually found mixing and dispensing potions, counting out capsules, and tapping powders out of larger bottles into smaller ones. While the pharmaceutical aspect accounts for the name of stores of this type, the whirl of customer activity was around the marbled soda fountain, in the center of the store. The syrup and soda dispensers gurgled and spurted as the "soda jerk" measured and mixed the wonderful drinks. Coca-Cola was "healthful" and Dr. Pepper was "delicious," and some thought both were medicinal. Ice cream was served in a clear glass dish. The leaded-glass combination light fixtures and dispensers accented both sides of the horseshoe-shaped counter and a beveled mirror around the square post in the center area reflected the lights and activity, making everything seem like it was happening twice. The stools, tables, and chairs were all of hardwood, constructed in a style that some people still refer to as "mission." On the backside of the center support post was a postcard rack that was readily available to those sitting nearby. While relaxing, one had a moment to share in the "postcard craze" by penning a quick message to a friend in another town or a beau who lived down the block.

273.   After the big fire of 1908 (card no 75), Joseph Huckins, Jr., proprietor of the Lee-Huckins Hotel, rebuilt an even finer and more extensive hotel on the same site at Main and Broadway. In order to capture the women's trade, one entire floor was reserved for ladies only, and included a special ladies' reception parlor. Here the starched window curtains and potted palms gave female guests a feeling of elegance and security in the new capital city. Mr. Huckins realized that this specialized service was unique and in order to gain maximum exposure he had this postcard published, along with others, to show off his new hotel.

274. Wicker furnishings were prevalent in this parlor area on the mezzanine of the Lee-Huckins Hotel. In a feature written by Bill Dutcher for **The Daily Oklahoman,** Joseph Huckins, Jr. was quoted as saying that his room clerks were "prepared to furnish button hooks, shoe horns, teaspoons, electric curling irons, ice and hot water bags, and numerous other articles."

This kind of attention was a specialty of the house for, as Huckins stated, "the average person away from home demands considerably more than a place to sleep." It was this desire to be of service that made the Lee-Huckins Hotel famous in the early days.

275. The Annex (card no. 74) was redesigned and opened in the early 1930's as a connecting garage to the Huckins Hotel, with the advertising slogan: "Drive Right Into the Huckins Hotel." Originally an extension with more hotel rooms, this seven-story garage held two hundred automobiles, and guests were able to drive in, register, and be taken at once to their rooms. By the time this postcard was published, the hotels were probably starting to feel the competition of the auto courts and early motels that permitted people easy access to their automobiles. At the Huckins you had the best of both worlds, and had the advantage of being near the center of downtown Oklahoma City as well.

276. The Albany Hotel, at 116½ South Hudson, was established some time in 1909 with Gustave Burcheardt as proprietor. Downstairs, at 116, was the Albany Cafe. This photographic postcard was probably taken soon after the opening of the hotel. The Albany was typical of many smaller hostelries found in the downtown area which catered to a lower-income clientele. Over the years there were many name changes, and at various periods the hotel was known as the Farris Flats, the Garrett Rooms, the Cline Hotel, and the Alexander Hotel. In later years the Albany Cafe became a religious mission, a soft drink emporium, and finally a bar, the Mexicali. The structure survived into the 1970's, but was demolished during the Urban Renewal period.

277. The Ohio Hotel, 114 North Harrison, opened its doors around 1915 under the management of Arnold Hangartner. It was a small, out-of-the-way hotel, but, judging from the throngs of people gathered around the entrance in this view, was not lacking in popularity. At the time of its opening, Harrison Avenue, lined with stately Victorian residences, was quite fashionable. Gradually, over the years, the wealthy moved elsewhere and the street became heavily commercialized. In 1938, the name of the hotel was changed to the Del Prado, which it has retained for the past forty-five years. Today it stands somewhat forlornly amid crumbling buildings and weed-filled vacant lots, but residents still watch the passing scene from the front porch.

COFFEE SHOP — SKIRVIN HOTEL — OKLAHOMA CITY, OKLA.

278. An extensive renovation at the Skirvin Hotel, carried out in 1930, raised all three wings to fourteen floors, doubled the lobby space, and added the coffee shop that is shown in this postcard view. The April 20, 1930 issue of **The Daily Oklahoman** noted "the decorations are the latest of modernistic design. Lighting fixtures, counter designs, windows and ceilings all carry out this keynote. Seating capacity is 300, with counter service to accommodate 80 persons, offering prompt service to those who have but a few minutes for their meal." An "iced-air system" pulled in air from far above the street level, forced it in through frosted coils and blew it into the coffee shop through 14 panels at the rate of 40,000 cubic feet per minute. The Skirvin's many patrons undoubtedly enjoyed the comfort of this additional modern convenience.

THE VENETIAN ROOM — SKIRVIN HOTEL — OKLAHOMA CITY, OKLA.

279. The Venetian Room was part of the new rooftop garden added during the 1930 renovation of the Skirvin Hotel. Murals depicting Venetian scenes were created by local artist and decorator, Carl A. Schmeusser. The floor was made of alternating red and white oak blocks nine inches square, arranged to give a parquet effect, and polished to a mirror surface. Lighting was both direct — from suspended Venetian type lanterns — and indirect — from colored lights concealed around the ceiling line. Acoustical masonite and special paint were used on the ceiling for their sound-absorbing qualities. Nationally famous recording orchestras performed for supper dances and for a time some of the music was broadcast daily by radio station WKY.

280. The Oklahoma Club (card no. 72) was completed in 1922 at 202-208 West Grand and was a private club, admitting only members and their guests. Sometime in the late 1930's, the Flamingo Room was opened in the main dining room on the second floor. The tables were arranged around huge square pillars which bordered the dance floor. A platform for musicians was next to the wall. One former guest remembers that the Flamingo Room was a very formal and elegant place. She also recalls that the specialty of the house was a distinctive mushroom sauce which was lavishly spread on the juicy steaks served here.

281. On the thirtieth floor of the First National Building (card no. 210) was the Rainbow Room, famous for its fine dining and superb panoramic view of Oklahoma City. Its advertising boasted that it was "400 feet in the clouds." A wonderful dance floor and an area for live musical entertainment were among its drawing features. One lady remembers the Rainbow Room as the place her husband took her for dinner and dancing on the evening of his return from World War II. It was a swanky place! In business for less than a decade, the Rainbow Room was first listed in the telephone directory in June, 1943, and last listed in the September, 1948 edition.

282. The Fine Foods Restaurant, 330 West Grand, had its entrance on the ground floor of the Rex Hotel. To accommodate its customers, there were three rows of booths and a counter for quick service. The owner, Pete Stamatis, opened for business sometime in mid-1946, with the motto "Service and Quality." A former patron recalls that she favored the hamburger steak. Fine Foods was last listed in the 1949 telephone book, so it is assumed that it closed about that time. Many of the downtown restaurants were open round-the-clock to serve workers getting off from graveyard shifts throughout the city. Much of this increased round-the-clock activity began during World War II and continued in the post-war years.

283. The eleven-story Hotel Black on the northwest corner of Grand and Hudson was completed in 1930 by Lucian Black. It was constructed at a cost of $600,000 with an additional $85,000 spent on furnishing the two hundred rooms, each with bath. The exterior finish was called modernistic at the time, but today is more commonly referred to by architectural historians as Native American-Art Deco. Along the top there was an intricate combination of buff brick with darker-colored brick for trimming, together with white stone and colored tile that together formed geometric patterns reminiscent of Native American designs. Guest prices ranged from two to three dollars per day, making the Black competitive with the other fine hotels of the city.

HOTEL LAWRENCE

Oklahoma City's Newest and Most Modern Hotel situated in the center of the Business and Theatre Districts. Convenient to all Stations and Car Lines.

RATES: $1.00 and Up. 75 Rooms with Bath.

284 RARDIN and O. S. FOWLER, Managers.

the
Roberts
hotel
OK285HOMA CITY, OKLAHOMA

284. The Hotel Lawrence was completed in 1912 and at 17 West Grand, was indeed "situated in the center of the business and theatre districts." This postcard view illustrates an advertising technique that was not at all uncommon: taking a photograph and air-brushing out the other buildings alongside (in this case the Hotel Kingkade on the Lawrence's west side is missing), making the advertiser appear more important. Local legend tells of the state supreme court operating from the sixth floor of the Hotel Lawrence, during the time when its own chambers were under construction northeast of town.

285. Sometime during its forty-five year history, the Wells-Roberts Hotel dropped the first part of its original name and became the Roberts Hotel. Explosives demolished the Roberts on January 14, 1973 . . . finally! The blast went off on schedule, but for ten minutes and forty seconds the building seemingly remained intact; then, in an instant the hotel came down in a cloud of dust. Although the steel framework had been cut with explosives, the brick walls had accepted the strain and supported the building. However, in the end, they gave way in a spectacular collapse.

286. Built in 1927, the Wells-Roberts Hotel opened for business in 1928 at 15 North Broadway. Tulsa financiers E. L. Wells and C. L. Roberts were the original owners, investing more than $400,000 in the ten-story structure. Oklahoma City's hotel capacity was increased by more than two hundred rooms when the Wells-Roberts opened as a first-class, moderately-priced hotel. This view shows the attractive front desk and lobby area.

Lobby, Wells Robert Hotel, Oklahoma City, Okla.

286

K4242

287

OKLAHOMA BILTMORE — OKLAHOMA CITY

288

287. The Oklahoma Biltmore was without a doubt one of the finest hotels in the post-oil boom days of Oklahoma City. There were 619 rooms, each offering free radio, circulating ice water, ceiling fans with up-and-down draft, and, later, air conditioning. In 1936 the Biltmore was headquarters for 104 conventions, served 284,604 meals, and had 114,171 guests! H. P. "Johnnie" Johnson, manager, always said in the advertising, "On your next visit to the Oil Capital be sure to register at the Biltmore."

288. On October 16, 1977 the Hotel Biltmore was demolished by a team of demolition specialists. Hundreds of low-yield explosives were planted throughout the building so that it would collapse and fall inward into an acceptable area only slightly larger than the hotel's foundation. The purpose was both to break the materials into smaller pieces that would be easily transported away, and to contain the blast and debris within the area, in order to minimize damage to surrounding structures. The razing was recorded by hundreds of camera buffs.

SIEBER HOTEL — NORTH HUDSON AT TWELFTH — OKLAHOMA CITY, OKLAHOMA

289. Records indicate that the Sieber Hotel, one of the first apartment hotels built in the city, was completed in the summer of 1928. Built by Swiss immigrant and grocer Robert G. Sieber at Twelfth and Hudson, the structure cost about $250,000. The hotel has sixty-five single rooms, six one-bedroom apartments, and mine efficiencies. The Sieber has changed owners several times and in 1978 underwent extensive remodeling, including the installation of new carpeting and repainting of the woodwork. Its near downtown location is ideal for housing students, retirees, and families with members being treated at nearby medical centers.

290. The El Rancho Tap Room opened for business in early 1945 and soon thereafter published this postcard, probably to give away to its customers. Judging from the signs painted on the walls, it seems safe to assume that it catered to a clientele mostly made up of servicemen and women: "Welcome Waves!" "Welcome M. P.'s and S. P.'s, Browse Around A While" "Is Everybody Happy?" "Everybody Welcome Except the Following: Undesirables, Chiselers, Gigolos, and Hooligans." Remembered for its comfortable booths, deluxe service, and the coldest beer in town, the El Rancho inhabited its 410 North Broadway address until sometime in 1968, when it closed its doors permanently.

291. The Britling Cafeteria was just east of the Civic Center (card no. 230), at 221 West First. In the September 13, 1939 issue of the **Oklahoma City Times,** a large illustrated ad announced the Britling's fall and winter fare. For breakfast one could order fresh orange juice for 10¢, hot biscuits for 1¢ each, hot muffins for 2¢ each, and cereals, either hot or cold, were 5¢. Serious eaters might order one large fresh egg any style, two strips of bacon, hominy grits, and ham gravy — all for 7¢; or, three large hot cakes with pure maple syrup or a crispy waffle with syrup for 9¢. Each Thursday night was "Courtesy Night" when every guest was served complimentary ice cream and cake. An added attraction was dinner music by Clarence Tackett and his orchestra, featuring Miss Millie Imel, vocalist, from 6:15 to 7:15.

292. The Classen Cafeteria opened for business in mid-1948 at 2400 Classen Boulevard, previously the first home of O'Mealey's, which had moved to its Northwest Twenty-third address (card no. 293). Ralph Geist was the owner of the Classen Cafeteria and it soon became famous for two specialties — its chicken pie and pastries. Located in a residential area that was beginning to turn commerical, the Classen Cafeteria prospered for nearly two decades. It offered good food at fair prices and attractive dining facilities. Sometime in 1967 the Classen closed and for a time the building was vacant. Today the Soul Boutique occupies the space.

YOUR RESIDENTIAL
Cafeteria

WHERE U. S. HIGHWAY NO. 66 CROSSES THE FAMOUS
CLASSEN BOULEVARD AT TWENTY - THIRD STREET
OKLAHOMA CITY

293. The O'Mealey family has been in the cafeteria business for several decades beginning in the 1940's when they opened at 2400 Classen Boulevard. This location later became the Classen Cafeteria (card no. 292). By 1952 there were three locations: O'Mealey's State Capitol Cafeteria, one at 319-321 Northwest Twenty-third, and another at 3132 North May. Gradually the operations were reduced to the North May address. This postcard, from the Twenty-third Street location, was picked up as the patron paid $5.08 for a meal for four people, or $1.27 for each person. The patron wrote on the backside, "Service excellent — cheapest food on trip to date."

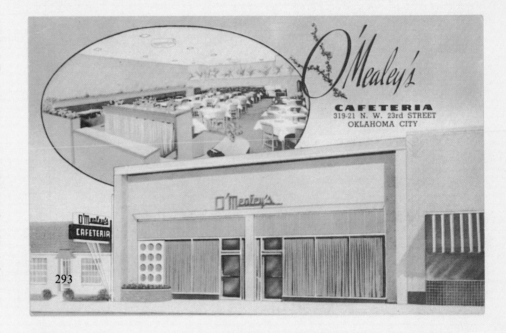

O'Mealey's
CAFETERIA
319-21 N. W. 23rd STREET
OKLAHOMA CITY

294. Flowers were in abundance on that day in 1947 when the Boulevard Cafeteria first opened with owner-manager Garland B. Arrington in charge. This earliest location was at Tenth and Classen Boulevard, opposite the Plaza Court. The Boulevard has long been known for its good food and pleasing decor. On June 2, 1976, it moved to a new location at 525 Northwest Eleventh and it continues to operate there today. The Classen address eventually became the Queen Ann Cafeteria, but today the building is vacant. Cafeterias have proved to be popular with an ever-wider audience through the years, and the idea of "going through the salad bar" has been accepted from roadside eateries to fine dining rooms throughout the nation.

BOULEVARD CAFETERIA

— DELICIOUS FOOD —
DELIGHTFUL SURROUNDINGS
ON CLASSEN BOULEVARD
OPPOSITE PLAZA COURT
OKLAHOMA CITY, OKLAHOMA

295.   Owned and managed by the Alvarado family, the El Charro Cafe was located on the corner of Tenth and Dewey. Guests were invited to enter either the main dining room shown at the top of this postcard, or the Maya Club Room in the lower part of the card. Total seating capacity was 250. Interesting murals throughout the cafe gave an atmosphere of culture south of the border.

296.   The Alvarado family also owned the Cafe El Charrito at 2909 Paseo, in the heart of the "Spanish Village." A companion to the El Charro (card no. 295), it served the best Mexican foods. It had a special Fiesta Room that was available for parties, but reservations were suggested. The owners were also affiliated with the Cafe Palacio at 3325 South Robinson and also the El Charro Cafe in Wichita, Kansas.

297.   Who could forget the giant fish encircled by the neon sign on top of Herman's! It was located on the northwest corner of Classen and Sixteenth Street. Mr. and Mrs. Herman Baggett first owned a small cafe at 500 North Hudson, and sometime in 1950 moved to the larger location shown here. The menu was a board in the shape of a fish. There were oysters on the half shell, and every dish was fresh and good. On one side of the restaurant was a fish market. Herman's would dip the fish in cornmeal, if you wished, or in their special preparation which was strong with paprika. By 1977 Herman's had closed. Today, Triple's Restaurant occupies the site.

298. The El Fenix Restaurant, with the "finest in Mexican food" was on the northeast corner of Broadway and Twenty-second Street at 2300 North Broadway. It was in business at this location from 1951 through 1955, on the same site previously occupied by Garland's Drive-In (card no. 304). Serving American and seafood dishes in addition to its south-of-the-border specialties, the El Fenix offered a private dining room and had plenty of free parking. Reservations were encouraged. After the business closed in 1955, the name was not used again until 1974 when an El Fenix opened in the new Crossroads Mall.

299, 300. The story is told that in 1921 Beverly Osborne borrowed $15.00 from his milkman, pawned his wife's engagement ring, sold his car, and opened a six-stool waffle shop on West Grand, offering 19¢ meals. Serving at full capacity he was able to make his payments, redeem his wife's ring, pay back the milkman, and buy another restaurant. While driving on a vacation, Beverly and his wife Rubye hit a bump and the chicken they were eating spilled on the floor. Her reaction was to laugh and say, "This is chicken in the rough." Her statement sparked an idea and soon Beverly's was serving half a fried chicken on a platter with shoestring potatoes, hot rolls with honey, but with no silverware.

His trademark became a cigar-smoking rooster with a golf bag and broken club, searching for a ball in the rough. This rooster, along with the concept and slogan "Chicken in the Rough," was franchised at more than 350 locations throughout the nation, and two foreign countries.

Metal finger buckets with the rooster on the side were on tables wherever "Chicken in the Rough" was served.

Card no. 299 shows the original Grill at 209 West Grand, Beverly's Gridiron at 1207 North Walker, and Beverly's Drive-In one block north of the State Capitol. All three restaurants are gone today, but the Beverly's name continues to be associated with the restaurant business in Oklahoma City including the one opened recently in the Exchange Building at the Stockyards.

Beverly Osborne fostered loyalty among his employees by sharing profits through bonuses and commissions. They in turn shared his enthusiasm as shown in card no. 300.

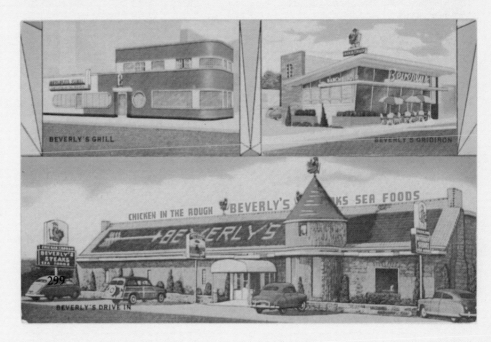

301. "When in Oklahoma City, Dine at Jean's, 117 West Twenty-third Street, where you will see a collection from the Southwest too wonderful for words to describe ... and meet Jean in person, who has a national reputation for serving Quality Food." Documentation is scarce on this restaurant, but apparently Jean's was in business for only a short time around 1929 or 1930. The restaurant featured a fascinating decor which included numerous hunting trophies, firearms hung from the ceiling, and at least one violin! Jean Van Almen was the proprietor and undoubtedly was a man who would have been interesting to know.

302. Glen Eaves' name has long been associated with fine dining in Oklahoma City at the original Glen's Hik-Ry Inn at 2815 Northwest Tenth, as well as at other locations around town. This view shows Glen's sometime in the 1950's, and while it has undergone extensive remodeling since then, it remains famous for its charcoal-broiled steaks. Glen's claim to fame is having been the first in the city to offer an "all-you-can-eat" smorgasbord for lunch. The promise continues "At Glen's Hik-Ry Inn an experience of delightful dining in wonderous surroundings awaits you."

303. George (nicknamed "Jeff") and Ruth Shilling first lived in this location in the early 1950's, and, within a few years, directory listings indicate they were selling poultry. Soon they were serving golden fried chicken dinners. The restaurant's external decor had a western theme, complete with a wagon wheel fence and the JR Ranch brand on the entrance gates. They feature family style dinners with their own home-raised fryers. The menu also offers choice cut steaks. Take-out fried chicken is also available for picnics and parties. Street renumbering in the 1960's resulted in an address change from 5640 to 5016 Northwest Tenth, where the restaurant still continue to do business.

304. "Tis the Taste that tells the Tale" ... this was the motto that Garland's Drive-In Restaurant at Twenty-second and Broadway used in its advertising. Garland B. Arrington founded the drive-in in 1939 and it remained at this location until 1950. The architecture depicted in this view has a certain Art Deco flavor in both the coloring and the design of the building. The decor inside was characterized by floral wallpaper and decorative wrought-iron fixtures. Garland's was know for its Tennessee Country Ham, Fried Chicken, and Corn Fed Steaks, as well as Individual Chicken Pies. It offered curb service and several people remember that whatever the total bill, the standard tip was 10¢, if you really wanted to "put on the dog."

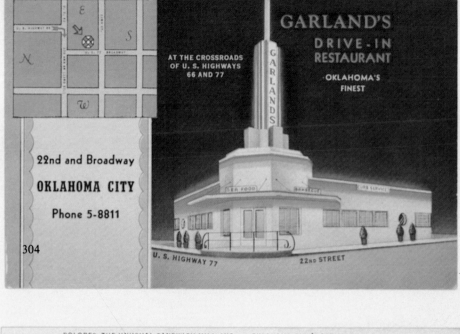

305. Dolores, "The Unusual Sandwich Mill," founded by Ralph A. Stephens, opened for business in February, 1930, at 33 Northeast Twenty-third Street. It featured drive-in facilities in the rear, important for folks who wanted to stick close to their fine automobiles. An early-day sandwich menu shows Goose Liver on rye at 15¢, Pimento Cheese at 20¢, and Baked Ham at 15¢. Unusual types of pies from its own bakeshop were offered at 10¢ per portion. Coffee was 5¢ and plain sundaes were 15¢, with nuts, 20¢. The business prospered: in 1937, and again in 1941, it was forced to expand. Late in 1974, however, Dolores closed its doors and the contents were sold at public auction on February 1, 1975.

306. Dinah's Bar-B-Que Restaurant, "The Original Home of Bar-B-Que Beans," was at 9014 North Western in the early to mid-1950's. Dinah's offered curb service as well as inside facilities for meals. Bar-B-Que was a specialty, along with sizzling steaks, fish, fried chicken, and sandwiches. Though Dinah's has long been out of business, the structure shown in this postcard looks nearly the same today and is currently the home of Baker's Printing.

BANK PACKING TOWN, OKLA. CITY OKLA.

307. This view pictures the Oklahoma Stock Yards National Bank Building on the northwest corner of Exchange and Agnew, in the middle of Packing Town. Hugo Weil's Cigar Store and the South Oklahoma Town Company were situated in the west end of the bank building. The bank was organized in 1910 with T. P. Martin, Jr. as its first president. E. F. Bisbee was the vice-president, and E. J. Kitteer the cashier. The streetcar tracks curved south along Agnew at this intersection, offering convenient transportation for packing plant workers. Today, this prime corner location is the site of the United Oklahoma Bank.

Swift & Company's Building, Oklahoma City.
D. H. Shenk Const. Co., Builders.
Faced with Cleveland
Round Edge Vitrified Brick.

308. J. P. Cannon was the manager of Swift and Company's operation when it moved in 1914 to this new brick structure at 2 East First Street. This location served as both the office and warehouse for an expanding business in Oklahoma City and the surrounding area. At this time Swift and Company dealt in meats, dairy products, poultry, and produce. The company was ideally situated near the downtown hotels, markets, and railroad facilities. Its last year in this building was 1973, and soon thereafter the structure was razed. The Dolese Company occupies the site today.

SCHWARZSCHILD & SULZBERGER COMPANY—HOG DRESSING.

309. The Schwarzschild & Sulzberger Company, also known as the S & S Co. (card no. 126), opened its packing plant in Oklahoma City in 1910. This recently discovered view, circa 1910, shows the new S & S meat processing assembly line. Farmers and ranchers brought cattle and hogs to the stockyards, where a livestock commission firm served as the middleman between the processors and suppliers. The animals were then slaughtered and dressed out and, within a few days, loaded aboard ice-refrigerated railroad cars for the trip to the east or west coast markets. The arrival of the packing plants in Oklahoma City gave a timely boost to the regional economy.

310. The Wilson & Co.'s meat packing plant, shown as a vignette in this postcard view, has been previously described (card no. 127), but it was the internationally famous six-horse Clydesdale team, part of the Wilson & Co.'s promotional package, which thrilled audiences wherever they appeared. Advertised as "Six Tons of Live Power," these champions came directly from the Texas Centennial to Oklahoma City in the fall of 1936 to be featured before the grandstand at the Oklahoma State Fair. The public participated by guessing how much the team weighed and entered the Wilson & Co.'s contest by picking up an entry form at its State Fair booth.

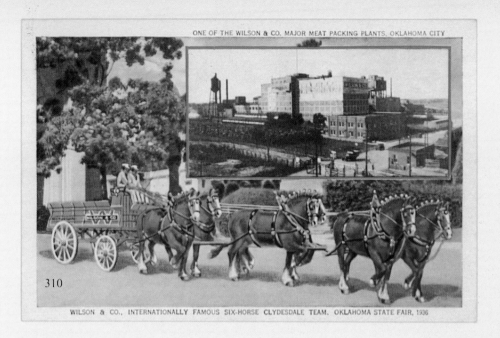

ONE OF THE WILSON & CO. MAJOR MEAT PACKING PLANTS, OKLAHOMA CITY

WILSON & CO., INTERNATIONALLY FAMOUS SIX-HORSE CLYDESDALE TEAM. OKLAHOMA STATE FAIR, 1936

311. On May 27, 1930, the original Coliseum (card no. 123) was consumed by fire; the new Coliseum shown here was built in its place. A boxing card was the entertainment for opening night, August 16, 1932. Livestock and 4-H shows, boxing, and wrestling were all regularly scheduled at the Coliseum. Shop owners along Agnew still recall the noise of the applause and cheers from fans at sports competitions. The lack of air conditioning, which was featured in the new arenas at the fairgrounds, drove promoters from the old to the new facilities. Closing its doors in 1970, the Coliseum was later demolished and a portion of the land utilized for the drive-in facility of the United Oklahoma Bank.

COLISEUM, OKLAHOMA CITY, OKLAHOMA

312. This view documents flood waters as they appeared on South Robinson Street and throughout the lower parts of the city on the morning of October 16, 1923. Everything happened so quickly, residents still recall, that the yellow torrent of water which had pushed over the North Canadian River bank around 2:00 a.m., had reached a point between California and Grand at Western Avenue by 4:30 a.m. Sirens sounded the alarm, warning some fifteen thousand residents south of Grand Avenue of the rampaging river.

South Robinson St. Tuesday, Oct 16th,

Flood water over City Dam. 313

313, 314, 315. Later that same morning Mayor O. A. Cargill issued a special proclamation to the citizens of Oklahoma City stating that "for the protection of property within the flood district, police and soldiers on duty have been ordered to shoot to kill any person found looting and breaking into any abandoned house or store building." Sightseers were barred, and in order to enter the flooded area, property owners were required to obtain a pass from the mayor's office or the police station. **The Daily Oklahoman** reported that these precautions were in response to the news reaching police that some seventy-five to a hundred men, believed to be hoboes, were looting homes in the vicinity of South Robinson and Pine (Tenth Street). Special deputies were soon on the scene and the wrongdoers dispersed.

Base Ball Park, OKLA City 314

View 313 shows the east end of the dam with the flood waters cascading over it. In the mist and darkness of the early morning, the crest of the North Canadian River washed through a gap some two hundred feet wide, ripping through steel reinforcing, concrete, dirt, and rock. For a broader perspective, refer to view 180. The breaks in the dam occurred on both sides of the red-roofed structure above the dam.

The flood interrupted the battle for the Western League pennant between the Oklahoma City Indians and the Tulsa Oilers that fall. The ruin of the Colcord Park baseball facilities, shown in view 314, illustrates why the teams were forced to move their play to a diamond near the State Fair grounds, east of the city. The Indians went ahead to win the pennant by a half-game margin.

Street Car Track to Capitol Hill. 315

Transportation to Capitol Hill and Packingtown was also interrupted; view 315 shows the damage to the streetcar tracks to Capitol Hill. The massive ties and steel rails were lifted and twisted by the tremendous force of the water.

Food and shelter were provided to the refugees by community leaders who assembled volunteers to man the relief stations, help with bread and coffee lines, and to arrange for shelter. The citizens rallied to the assistance of those who had suffered in this Great Flood of 1923.

316. "When I am governor, there will not be an inaugural ball. I am going to give an old fashioned square dance and barbecue. It will be a party for all the people and I want you all to come." So said the 1922 candidate for governor, John Calloway "Jack" Walton, as he stumped the state for votes. He won the election and "sure enough" gave a barbecue! Many thousands of Oklahomans flocked to the city for the inaugural on January 8, 1923, and to the parade and barbecue the next day. Old and young, rich and poor: they were all there for this tremendous party for the people. This view shows a scene at the fairgrounds.

317. Three of these boxcar-sized coffee urns were in place for the barbecue. They are said to have held 10,000 gallons and some accounts say that each one served 50,000 people. That is a lot of coffee! For the barbecue on Tuesday afternoon, the percolating of the coffee was begun on Monday, with the hot water heated by steam fire engines. The tops of several of these steam engines can be seen in this view. A carload of tin drinking cups in which to serve all of this coffee was donated. One can only imagine the taste or consistency of coffee brewed and served in this manner, but everyone here looks satisfied and that is what counts.

318. Governor-elect Walton was sworn into office before a joint session of the state legislature at the State Capitol on Monday, January 8, 1923. The following day, festivities began with a grand parade that formed at the stockyards and worked its way through downtown Oklahoma City and on east to the fairgrounds. Zack Mulhall was the marshal of the parade and he was followed by the team of three oxen pulling an old wagon which is shown in this view. Over 25,000 people were scheduled to participate in bands and marching units that represented various organizations, and still hundreds more were caught up in the spirit of things and just joined in line and made their way to the barbecue.

2595 Pilgrim Congregational Church, Oklahoma City, Ok.

319

319. The Congregational Church was organized in Oklahoma City on November 16, 1889. The first services were held in Mrs. Brown's Boarding House on the northeast corner of Hudson and California; later, gatherings were held in a feed store on the corner of Harvey and Southwest Third. Mrs. M. C. Nortte, one of the charter members of the church, donated lots on the northwest corner of Harvey and Southwest Fourth and over the years several frame buildings were built on this site before the Pilgrim Congregational Church, shown in this postcard, was constructed in 1904. Miss Edna Mae Lindsey is thought to have established the first kindergarten in the city in the basement of this church.

Park congregational Church
320

320. The Park Congregational Church, shown here, was built in the early 1920's, at 829 Northwest Thirteenth Street. Soon after it was constructed, the Congregationalists in the city unified and renamed this structure the Pilgrim Congregational Church. It was built of tan-colored brick with white stone trim. There was a four-cornered tower above each of the two entrances on the north side of this three-story building. A large oval-shaped window with five long narrow panels was placed between these two towers. In 1972 the building was sold and converted to office space and today, known as the 1433 Classen Building, it is occupied by legal, architectural, and construction firms. The congregation, meanwhile, has merged with Mayflower Congregational Church at 3901 Northwest Sixty-third.

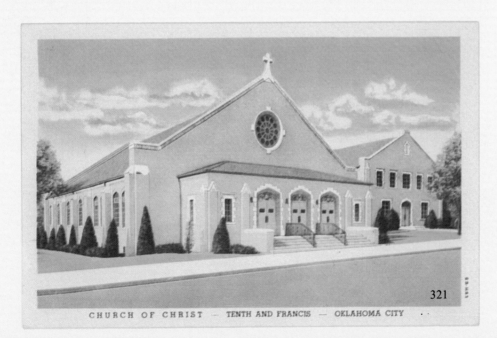

321

CHURCH OF CHRIST — TENTH AND FRANCIS — OKLAHOMA CITY

321. This church, located on the northwest corner of Northwest Tenth and Francis, was home for the first Church of Christ congregation in Oklahoma City. Prior to its construction in 1918, the members of the church had held services in the old County Court House. During its long history, it has been the "mother church" of several other Churches of Christ in the area. A few years ago, the members moved to a new location, 3536 Northwest Thirty-eighth Street, and adopted the name Broadview Heights Church of Christ. The old education building, to the right of the church in this view, has been converted to offices for a legal firm, and the sanctuary is now used as a gymnasium.

322. In 1945 the Corpus Christi Catholic Church was built at Sixteenth and Kelley. Rev. John J. Waldie was the parish priest and is remembered for his religious radio broadcasts. This church, with its two dissimilar bell towers, is considered an excellent example of Spanish Colonial Renaissance architecture. Corpus Christi parochial school is located east of the church.

323. The Pennsylvania Avenue Christian Church appears today much as it did in this postcard printed soon after it was built. Located on the northwest corner of Pennsylvania and Twelfth Street, it was dedicated on Sunday, May 24, 1925. The congregation was three years old at that time, and had been meeting elsewhere while its new church home was completed. In additon to a beautiful sanctuary, the building housed a fine dining hall and a Sunday School with departmental rooms for each age group. A modified Gothic architectural style was carried out in the construction of this church.

324. The Kelham Avenue Baptist Church first appears in the city directory at this location, Northeast Fourteenth and Kelham Avenue, in 1910. The text on the back of this postcard indicates that the church was reorganized in May, 1924 with Rev. R. C. Howard as its pastor. It goes on to assert, "Howard has drawn no salary during the years," and it can only be assumed that his livelihood was gained through his position as head of the Liberty National Life Insurance Company, which he held concurrent with his role as pastor. Around 1960 the church was sold and became the Avery Chapel, African Methodist Episcopal Church, one of the community's leading black churches.

KELHAM AVENUE BAPTIST CHURCH   OKLAHOMA CITY

PRESENT and PROPOSED BUILDINGS
CAPITOL HILL BAPTIST CHURCH
South Harvey from S. W. 24th to S. W. 25th Street
OKLAHOMA CITY, OKLAHOMA

325

325. The Capitol Hill Baptist Church, with twelve charter members, had its organizational service on the first Sunday in August, 1902. Its forerunner had been a portable tabernacle, located in the 200 block on old West A: from this street mission the Capitol Hill Baptist Church was founded. Its first pastor was C. L. Green. In 1903 its first building was erected and remained on A Street until 1923, when a new brick church was built on the corner of Commerce and Harvey. This remains its location today, and the church continues to expand.

Capitol Hill was founded as a city on May 3, 1904, and its first mayor was George Flannagan. The community was annexed to Oklahoma City in 1910.

DOWNTOWN BAPTIST CHURCH — OKLAHOMA CITY

326

326. The lettering on the front of this structure indicates that it was initially called the Main Street Arcade Building, but it has never appeared in any of the city directories by this name. Over the years, the building has housed an unusual range of occupants. In 1923 Hill's Business College and the Crescent Nut Company became tenants. Former customers of the nut company, which occupied one of the streetside locations, still recall the special hand-picked black walnut meats that were offered for sale. The Downtown Baptist Church, with its motto "Keep Them Coming," was established here in 1937. The location at 629 West Main Street, in the heart of Oklahoma City, allows the church to minister to the "throngs in the center of the city."

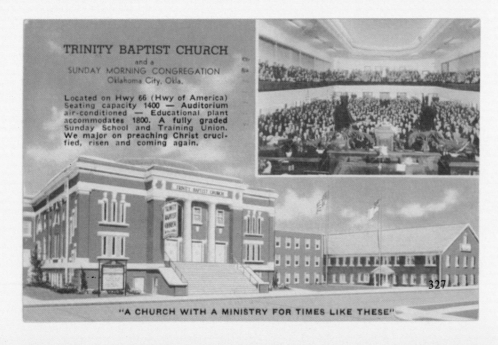

TRINITY BAPTIST CHURCH
and a
SUNDAY MORNING CONGREGATION
Oklahoma City, Okla.

Located on Hwy 66 (Hwy of America)
Seating capacity 1400 — Auditorium air-conditioned — Educational plant accommodates 1800. A fully graded Sunday School and Training Union. We major on preaching Christ crucified, risen and coming again.

327

"A CHURCH WITH A MINISTRY FOR TIMES LIKE THESE"

327. The Trinity Baptist Church, which began meeting in June, 1907 as a mission Sunday School of the First Baptist Church, was formally organized on May 1, 1911. The northeast corner of Northwest Twenty-third and Douglas has always been the church's location. When this postcard was mailed in 1949, the church was capable of seating 1,400, and had an air-conditioned auditorium. It has continued to grow and today has a membership of more than 4,000. Trinity Baptist is the "mother church" of Village, Mayfair, and Wheatland Baptist Churches.

328. The high school building shown in the upper left corner of this multi-view card was known as Irving School (card no. 68). The two-story frame Bryant School, erected in the middle of the block at 317 North Geary in 1901, was later razed and superseded by the brick building shown on card no. 333. Lincoln School, located at 1138 North Geary, on the southeast corner of Northeast Eleventh and Geary, was replaced by a new school building constructed in 1919 on the same site. This new facility, known as the Opportunity School, provided education for children with special needs. In 1926 the original Lincoln name was restored to this school, which is still open at the present time.

329. Willard (card no. 68) and Washington (card no. 134) schools were described in **The Vanished Splendor.** Jefferson, 2317 North Western, functioned as an elementary school for thirty years, from 1919, when it opened, until 1949. After this time the structure was used as a school administration building until 1955, when it was sold. The building was demolished to make room for the construction of the Citizens National Bank. Emerson and Washington schools share the distinction of being the first public schools built (1894) in the city. Both were eight-room, two-story brick buildings. Emerson was located at Northwest Seventh and Walker. In 1917, a huge fire leveled Emerson, and destroyed the records of the board of education which were stored there. A new elementary school was built in its place, but was closed in 1972, when the building was put into service as an adult education school.

330. The McKinley School, 1120 North Harvey, opened to admit grade school pupils in the fall of 1907, about the time of statehood. It was named in memory of the recently assassinated President William McKinley. Mrs. Laura Bradley is listed as having served as its first principal. The architectural design cannot be classified as any particular style, but rather is a mixture of Greek and Romanesque elements. This hand-colored postcard view was published by H. H. Clark (card no. 55), who owned a curio store downtown.

Public School Buildings.
Oklahoma City, Okla.

Published by The Vosburgh Book Store.

Public School Buildings.
Oklahoma City, Okla.

Published by The Vosburgh Book Store.

EUGENE FIELD SCHOOL, OKLAHOMA CITY, OKLA.

331. Designed by Layton and Smith, the Eugene Field School, at 1515 North Klein, opened its doors in 1910 and remained operational until it was closed in 1982. Current plans call for another school on this same site, also to be named Eugene Field. The same structure that is pictured on this postcard turns up on others, identified as the Monte Ne Building. Only one listing, in 1909, has been found for a building with this name. Speculation suggests that these views may have been mislabeled as a result of this building's having been used as a meeting place for the businessmen who formed the Oklahoma chapter of the Monte Ne resort near Monte Ne, Arkansas.

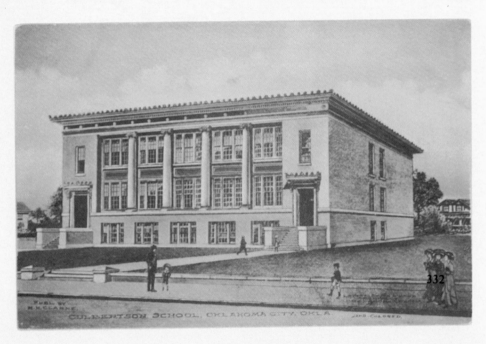

CULBERTSON SCHOOL, OKLAHOMA CITY, OKLA.

332. Although he never lived in Oklahoma City, J. J. Culbertson was an early investor in the area's property and generous with gifts that benefited the state and the community. He built the Culbertson Building (card no. 1), the city's first skyscraper, at Grand and Broadway. He is best remembered for donating, jointly with W. F. Harn, the land for the State Capitol and the governor's mansion. In conjunction with his son, J. J. Culbertson, Jr., a city resident, he developed the Culbertson Heights residential district, along with others. They deeded to the city the site at 1200 Northeast Thirteenth for the Culbertson School shown in this view. The school was constructed in 1909 and served the community until it was closed in 1977. The site is now occupied by the Oklahoma Medical Center.

Bryant School, Oklahoma City.

Layton-Smith, Architects, Oklahoma City.
J. G. Kennedy, Contractor, Oklahoma City.
Cleveland Vit. Brick Co.'s Round Edge Vitrified Face Brick used.

333. Bryant School was initially built as the two-story frame structure shown on card no. 328. This earlier building was razed and replaced by the handsome brick structure shown on this postcard in 1910. Built at a cost of $37,192, the school was designed by Layton and Smith, with J. G. Kennedy as the contractor. In 1934, the school's name was changed to Scarborough, only to be changed again to Inman Page School in 1937. The school closed in 1974, and soon thereafter was demolished. Today the site is a vacant lot.

334. Layton, Smith and Forsyth designed Harding Junior High School at 3333 North Shartel, and construction began in 1923. The school was named for President Warren G. Harding, who died in office on August 2, 1923. Streetcar tracks can be seen in the foreground, and trolleys undoubtedly transported some of the students to and from school. Additions were made to the original structure in 1926, 1930, and again in 1940, enlarging the plant to twenty-seven classrooms, an auditorium, cafeteria, and a gymnasium with a swimming pool. Harding, now called a "middle-school," still functions as an educational facility.

335. The Holmboe Company built Classen Junior High School, shown in this postcard view. Completed in 1919, the school was located at Eighteenth and North Ellison. Additions and improvements were made to the school and in time it became Classen Senior High School. Through the 1930's and 1940's the football rivalry between Central High School (card no. 135) and Classen High School was legendary and is remembered throughout central Oklahoma. The games were played in Taft Stadium, adjacent to Taft Junior High (card no. 336).

336. When construction began in 1930 for the $297,000 William Howard Taft Junior High School, there were complaints that it was "being built in the wilderness." Despite the critics, the placing of Taft Junior High School at 2901 Northwest Twenty-third Street proved to be a wise deicison, for within four years the school was crowded to capacity and an increasing enrollment forced additional classrooms to be built. There have been several more expansions through the years. The school is known for its 7,000-seat concrete stadium which has been the scene of countless sporting events for area teams.

337. When founded in 1916 by a group of physicians, all of whom were members of the First Baptist Church, the State Baptist Hospital had a twenty-five bed capacity. It became a denominational facility, called the Baptist Hospital, when it was bought by the church in 1922. The next year several doctors took over its ownership and changed the name to the Oklahoma General Hospital, and it was during this period that its image was preserved on this postcard view. Upon being purchased, in 1947, by the Sisters of Mercy, it was renamed Mercy Hospital-Oklahoma City General. The "General" was dropped from the name in 1968; and, in 1970, the institution was incorporated. In the early 1970's, Mercy Health Center moved from downtown to a site at Memorial Road and Meridian, leaving the building vacant.

HUBBARD HOSPITAL, OKLAHOMA CITY, OKLAHOMA

338. John C. Hubbard, M.D., began his medical practice in the city at Rolater's Hospital (card no. 142). When he was not included in an organizational staff hierarchy within Rolater's, Dr. Hubbard left to open his own Hubbard Hospital at 1501 Northeast Eleventh Street, on January 26, 1926. His was a "privately-owned, non-sectarian general hospital adhering strictly to the standard of hospital conduct as published by the American College of Surgeons, yet refusing to be dominated by the tenets of any one school of medical thought." The Hubbard Hospital prided itself on the splendid record of its obstetrical department. Originally a fine home, the hospital structure was remodeled several times, and later enlarged with a separate clinic building in 1952. The fine building shown in this view was razed after Dr. Hubbard passed away and the hospital ceased operation.

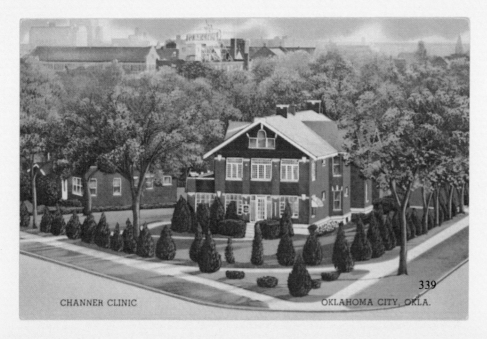

CHANNER CLINIC — OKLAHOMA CITY, OKLA.

339. Dr. Harold B. Channer was the founder of the Channer Health Clinic, initially located in the old Herskowitz home (card no. 370), at 711 Northwest Eleventh Street. Here he offered X-ray and fluoroscope examination, radionics, pathoclast, physiotherapy, colon therapy, and laboratory analysis. Later, Dr. Channer moved to 1329 Classen Boulevard (Drive), the clinic that is shown in this postcard view. The advertising stated, "The Channer Clinic is modern with every facility for diagnosis and treatment." In the background St. Anthony Hospital (card no. 140) can be seen. The Channer Clinic stands empty today.

340. This structure was originally an apartment house named the Wyatt Flats, but sometime in the mid-1920's, Dr. Earl D. McBride opened his Reconstruction Hospital and McBride Clinic here. Dr. McBride was an orthopedic surgeon and was a specialist in bone and joint diseases. The McBride Reconstruction Hospital was located at 717-723 North Robinson, and remained here until 1938. This building was demolished in June, 1983. Today, the McBride Clinic is located at 1111 North Dewey.

RECONSTRUCTION HOSPITAL & McBRIDE CLINIC — 717 to 723 North Robinson — Oklahoma City, Okla.

341. When constructed in 1931, this building was called the Capitol Hill Hospital and Clinic. It was sold in 1932 and the new owners renamed it the Samaritan Hospital. Later, it had still other owners, and, in 1942, became the Capitol Hill General Hospital. This linen postcard was distributed after the last name change. The building displays unusual architectural ornamentation along the cornice, which might be described as Native American motifs. This hospital fulfilled a vital need for many years, but eventually closed. Renovation plans are rumored, but the fate of the structure is uncertain.

342. The Polyclinic Hospital opened in 1929 on the northwest corner of Thirteenth and Robinson. The facility is well described on the back of this postcard: "A beautiful new, fireproof building, elaborately furnished and equipped with every modern facility to insure perfect service. A select staff of graduate nurses (no training school), every ward and room is well ventilated, most of which have south windows. All have electric ceiling fan, radio, telephone, night light, and better beds than your own. Rates in keeping with those of the other hospitals." With the same address, 209 Northwest Thirteenth Street, the institution is known today as Doctors General Hospital.

POLYCLINIC HOSPITAL, THIRTEENTH AND ROBINSON, OKLAHOMA CITY, OKLA.

PASTEUR MEDICAL BUILDING — Oklahoma City

343.

343. The Pasteur Medical Building, at the corner of Northwest Tenth and Lee, was opened to medical tenants in 1952. With free off-street parking for all patients and doctors, air conditioning throughout, good lighting, and automatic elevator service, the new facilities appealed to many doctors who were looking for a better location. Many residents will recall one of the early occupants, Dr. Ray M. Balyeat, whose practice was devoted exclusively to the diagnosis and treatment of allergies. The Pasteur Medical Building is still providing office space for area physicians.

CRIPPLED CHILDREN'S HOSPITAL, OKLAHOMA CITY, OKLA.—62

344

344. The Crippled Children's Hospital was described in the September 1, 1929 issue of **The Daily Oklahoman** as being like a "fairyland." Well-lighted rooms with walls of glass — one gaily decorated as a Moro castle — appealed to the children. Fairy tale characters marched along the brightly colored tile walls of some of the other rooms. Visitors were impressed with the scrupulous cleanliness, the complete range of services, "frigidaire fountains" in all the halls. The most unusual feature of the building was that the second and third floors were set back in a stairstep arrangement, thus providing sun porches on each floor. Located on Thirteenth Street, just east of the University Hospital, the Crippled Children's Hospital was completed in 1928 at a cost of $425,000. Today the facility is known as Oklahoma Children's Memorial Hospital.

UNIVERSITY HOSPITAL, OKLAHOMA CITY, OKLA.

345

345. In this view, looking southeast across the streetcar tracks on Thirteenth Street, the State University Hospital is shown. It was constructed of red brick with white stone trim in 1919 at a cost of $276,000. Two large Doric columns graced each side of the north entrance. Today, University Hospital is known as Oklahoma Memorial Hospital, and occupies a prominent place among the sprawling medical complexes which surround it. However, it has been so extensively remodeled and enlarged that it bears little resemblance to the older building in this view.

346. The Variety Club Health Center, at 600 South Hudson, was dedicated in June, 1941. Maintained by the Oklahoma Variety Club, a service organization, the purpose of the center was to render, to the needy, complete clinical and medical service under the supervision of the Oklahoma County Health Association. For those who were unable to pay for private medical and dental services, help was provided in these areas: dental care, tuberculosis treatment, maternal and child health, eye care, X-ray and laboratory services, mobile X-ray clinics, and health information. The help rendered by this center through the years has been immeasurable. The Variety Health Center, Inc. is now located at 1504 South Walker.

VARIETY CLUB HEALTH CENTER Oklahoma City, Okla.

347. To capture this scene the photographer climbed to the top of the Pioneer Telephone Building (card no. 85) and aimed his camera north along Broadway. An interesting comparison may be made between this 1910 view and the earlier one on card no. 86. The Broadway Hotel had been built in the foreground, and the long shadow falling across Broadway on the right is from the recently completed Oklahoma Publishing Company Building (cards no. 30 and 211). The three towers in the background were connected with the building of Central High school (card no. 135), which was under construction at this time. Broadway was changing from residential to commercial status.

348. According to library source materials, Mr. and Mrs. W. B. Goudelock sold their residence at 1021 West Sixteenth Street in 1929. Soon thereafter the house became the offices of The Oklahoma Life Insurance Company, with Bert Smith as president, and William S. Key and James C. Smith as vice-presidents. The firm is listed for this address for only two years, and, by 1933, the Pyramid Life Insurance Company and the Middle States Royalty Corporation occupied the property. Today, the structure is known as the Freeman Building, and contains the offices of several attorneys.

OKLAHOMA LIFE INSURANCE COMPANY — OKLAHOMA CITY

349. Captain Daniel Stiles, one of the "founding fathers" of Oklahoma City, began construction of this home at 611 Northeast Eighth Street in 1900. His widow sold the home to C. G. Jones in 1903 after her husband's death. This was an imposing structure with numerous rooms, a basement, fireplace, and distinctive turret, but only one bathroom! The Jones' telephone number was 5, signifying their residence was one of the first to have this new convenience. After Jones' death the home was sold to the Catholic Church and it was used for a time as a convent and later as a maternity home and nursery. In the mid-1950's, it was subdivided into apartments and then demolished around 1970.

350. This attractive home with a woman on the porch was at 22 Northwest Eighth Street. Aerial photographs taken in 1955 reveal that the house was still standing at that time, but it has since been razed. In the background one of the sheds belonging to the Gloyd Lumber Yard is visible. S. M. Gloyd came to Oklahoma in the late 1890's and over the years established himself as a successful lumber dealer throughout Oklahoma and Indian Territory.

351. The property at 1414 North Hudson was purchased by Alonzo Key, who began building this home in 1913. When only partially completed, Key sold it to General Roy Hoffman, who finished it and moved in sometime in 1915. This distinctive Spanish-style residence was designed by Henry C. Pelton of New York. The entrance is through the arched portico shown in this view, and gives access to a Spanish court two stories high. The living room is to the left, the dining area to the right, with the library straight ahead in the rear of the home. The court has a marble floor and a double stairway rises to a second floor balcony with its adjoining rooms. This postcard view, which shows the home soon after it was completed, features a sporty electric automobile out front with two passengers posing.

352. The Lorraine Apartments, situated on the southwest corner of Northeast Sixth and Central, was built shortly after statehood. The unusual neo-classical architectural plans called for placing elegant Ionic porticos at each corner of the building which faced a street, and this, combined with other features, resulted in the creation of a particularly handsome apartment house. The Lorraine Apartments survived into the 1970's, when, having fallen into a sad state of disrepair, they were demolished.

353. Mislabeled on the face of this postcard, this view is actually looking toward the northwest, at the intersection of Northeast Park and Central. The house on the far right, which is still standing at 229 East Park, was once the home of O. A. Mitscher, the mayor of Oklahoma City from 1892 until 1894. Mitscher was the father of Admiral Marc Mitscher, task force commander in the Battle of Midway (1942), and, later, Commander-in-Chief of the Pacific forces in World War II.

Note: Since the following ten recently discovered H.H. Clarke postcards are all circa 1910, the directory for that year was used to identify residents.

354. In this scene the viewer is looking northwest along Tenth Street from its intersection with Hudson. In 1910, two prominent physicians lived in the first two houses on the left: Dr. J. A. Ryan at 400 West Tenth; and Dr. William E. Dicken, surgeon for the Missouri, Kansas & Texas Railroad, at 410 West Tenth. Only vacant lots mark the location of these two homes today. Five forms of transportation are seen here: the electric car, the gasoline powered automobile, walking, the bicycle, and the horse-drawn buggy.

355. These three substantial homes once made up the entire north side of the 500 block of Northeast Eleventh Street. They were numbered from left to right as 501, 505, and 509. Each one had a distinctive style and they are certainly unlike anything being built today in developments where everything looks the same. Across the street to the south was Lincoln School (card no. 328), which the children from these homes undoubtedly attended. Built around the time of statehood, nothing remains of this block today except the sidewalk and stairsteps which led up to the 501 address on the left.

356. This was the 400 block on Northwest Thirteenth Street. The first house on the left, 433 Northwest Thirteenth, was the residence of Anton H. Classen, who was involved in developing both Epworth College and the streetcar system in the city. George B. Stone's home was at 425, in the middle of this view. He was the president of the Stone Realty Company. The third structure, at 421 Northwest Thirteenth, partially hidden by the trees, belonged to Charles F. Colcord. The Colcord home was torn down in January, 1965, and the property is now occupied by the offices of the Standard Life and Accident Insurance Company.

357. This hand-colored postcard shows the 700 block on Northwest Fourteenth Street around 1910. The first home to the left, numbered 723, was the residence of Solomon Barth, who, with Joseph Myer, had the Barth and Myer clothing store at 214-216 West Main Street. The red-roofed white home next door, numbered 721, belonged to William Mee, president of the Security National Bank (card no. 207).

358. This is a view of Northwest Fifteenth Street looking east from Shartel. The large home in the left foreground has long since disappeared, and another has been built in its place. However, the next house to the right is still standing on the northwest corner of Fifteenth and Lee. Both of these homes were built in the early part of this century in what is now known as Heritage Hills. This entire area of stately homes has been designated a Historical Preservation District.

359. This scene shows the middle of the 500 block of Northwest Fifteenth Street, looking west toward Dewey and the 600 block. Frank C. Chesley, secretary of the Oklahoma Fire Insurance Company in 1910, resided to the immediate left at 524 Northwest Fifteenth. Across the street west, at 600 Northwest Fifteenth, was the dwelling where Robert H. Gardner and his family lived. Mr. Gardner was a partner in the Pryer-Gardner Company, a real estate and investment firm. This home is still standing and is distinctive for its four very massive pillars and for the attractive flowers that bloom in the summertime along the sidewalk.

360. Attorney Rudolph A. Kleinschmidt lived in the home to the left in this view, at 628 Northwest Sixteenth Street. He had offices in the Insurance Building (card no. 47).His neighbors at 632, next door to the west, were George A. Todd and Hugh H. Todd and their wives. George Todd was president and Hugh Todd was manager of the Oklahoma Refining Company. Across the street, on the southwest corner of the intersection, at 700 Northwest Sixteenth, was the residence of William B. Skirvin, founder of the Skirvin Hotel and father of Pearl Mesta.

West Seventeenth Street. OKLAHOMA CITY, Okla.

361

361. The trees were mere saplings in this circa 1910 scene of Northwest Seventeenth Street. Years later they grew larger and made an arch over the street, providing shade and protection to these well-built homes. Along the north side of the street from North Lee, the second house from the corner with the red roof (705), belonged to Mose Baum, who, along with Marx Baum, owned a ladies outfitters' store in their namesake Baum Building (card no. 48) at Grand and Robinson. The 709 residence was Meyer Benson's, president of Benson's Ltd., a secondhand clothing store at 107 West Main. Merton A. Hassenflue, an insurance agent, lived at 711. Living in 719 was Joseph C. McClelland, president of the Tradesmens State Bank.

West 19th Street. OKLAHOMA CITY, Okla.

362

362. Also showing the north side of the 700 block, this residential scene is two blocks north of the previous view on Northwest Nineteenth Street. The porch post and roof is all that is visible of the 711 address to the far right, the home of Charles S. McPherson, bookkeeper. Next door, at 713, was the home of James F. Harbour, who is remembered with his partner W. M. Longmire for their popular furniture company. The three-story home (715) belonged to Ralph F. Parmenter, a partner in the Parmenter-Roersma Drug Co. The 717 address was vacant in 1910, and 721 belonged to real estate man George V. McClintic. Windpower was still in vogue, as the lone windmill testifies. Today these houses face Mesta Park across the street to the south.

363

North Shartell Street. OKLAHOMA CITY, Okla.

363. This circa 1910 view shows Northwest Seventeenth Street, as someone would see it looking west from its intersection with Shartel. Note the misspelling of "Shartel" on the card. This residential scene, as well as many others dating from the same era, shows a variety of styles and designs used in construction, which makes this neighborhood architecturally interesting. Many of these homes were custom-built to the owners' specifications, and reflected their individual tastes. The eighth home down the street, nearly hidden by trees, was the residence of the famous criminal attorney, Moman Pruiett. He was a member of the legal firm of Taylor, Pruiett, and Sniggs. His next door neighbor to the west was John M. Remington, president of the Remington Drug Co. (cards no. 271 and 272).

364. Bishop William A. Quayle served as Bishop of Oklahoma with the Methodist Episcopal Church for several years beginning in the fall of 1908, and during his tenure lived in this home. Located on the northeast corner of Eighteenth and Olie, the address was 931 Northwest Eighteenth Street. The residence returned to private ownership when Bishop Quayle was transferred to another area. The home is still standing, although its appearance has been altered and it is now surrounded with large trees.

365. What an intriguing home! Just imagine dashing up and down in this crenellated tower, the principal feature of this unusual residence. Architects refer to something like this as an "architectural conceit," for it cannot be attributed to a specific era or a recognized style, but rather is distinctive for its flamboyance and striking appearance. This was the home of the noted attorney, Russell N. McConnell, who became successful specializing in corporate and commercial law. His home was on the southeast corner of the Sixty-third and Western intersection, just east and across the street from the old University Heights Elementary School. Though the McConnells lived far north of town, they were conveniently near the interurban line on Classen Boulevard, which went south to Oklahoma City, or north to Edmond and Guthrie.

R. N. McConnell's Home, Oklahoma City, Okla.

366. It is doubtful if L. D. Kight ever lived in this residence at 1319 North Shartel, though he did build it and certainly sold it to a home buyer. Mr. Kight was the head of a prominent real estate firm and sold property throughout Oklahoma City. He was associated with O. P. Workman, A. H. Classen, and C. E. Bennett, as a principal stockholder in the Linwood Place Development Company, which built the residential section in northwest Oklahoma City called Linwood Place. This home has been converted into office space for a group of attorneys.

L. D. Kight, Owner
Oklahoma City, Okla.
Stewart & Wilderson,
Designers and Builders

CURTIS MILLWORK USED

W. T. Hale Residence, Oklahoma City, Okla.

367. Roy Stewart wrote in **Born Grown** that William T. Hales was not only a banker and real estate developer, but, at one time, was also the city's largest property owner. Designed by architects Hawk and Parr, the palatial Hales' residence was constructed in 1916 at 1521 North Hudson. Building materials, imported from Greece, insured a truly classic structure. After Mr. Hales passed away in 1939, the home was sold to the Roman Catholic Diocese of Oklahoma, and was, until recently, the residence of the Catholic bishops. The property, located in Heritage Hills, was placed on the National Register of Historic Places in 1973.

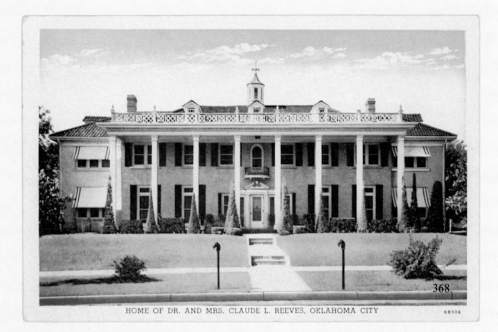

HOME OF DR. AND MRS. CLAUDE L. REEVES, OKLAHOMA CITY

368. The "Martha Washington" was built by homebuilders Callaway, Carey & Foster at 601 East Fourteenth Street and was placed on the Memorial Day tour in May, 1930. The advertising stated: "this home traces its architectural lineage to Mount Vernon, famous residence of our first president, but it has been modernized to conform to the living requirements of 1930. The rarest woods, the finest imported tiles and fixtures, the most appropriate hardware obtainable in the world, all have been blended into what critics declare to be the finest and most thoroughly-constructed home ever offered for sale in Oklahoma City." The Martha Washington continues to stand as a landmark today.

369. O. P. Workman's new $12,000 residence, built in the suburban Linwood Addition of Oklahoma City, was the talk of the town for several months in early 1911. The two-story home was designed by Layton, Smith and Hawk, Architects, and constructed by L. G. New and Son. Located at 3205 Northwest Nineteenth Street, the home was three and one-half miles from the business district and situated along the Linwood streetcar line. The woodwork on the first floor was quarter-sawn red oak and all of the doors were French style. There was a large reception room in the central portion of the first floor, and a grand staircase leading from the living room to the second story. Three bed chambers, each with its own fireplace, and two baths occupied the second story. Mr. Workman was the founder of the Workman Real Estate Company.

Residence, Linwood Addition. OKLAHOMA CITY, Okla.

370. Mrs. Max Herskowitz, the widow of the early merchant and proprietor of the Herskowitz Building (card no. 43), built this home at 711 Northwest Eleventh Street. Stewart and Wilderson were the general contractors and the residence is said to have cost $20,000 in 1912. Dark red vitrified brick with stone trimmings was used on the exterior and variegated tiling on the roof and porches. On the first floor there was a large living room, dining room, and breakfast area, with oak-beamed ceilings and colonnades and wainscotting of polished oak. Four bedrooms were upstairs, each with a private bath. After Mrs. Herskowitz passed away the home housed the Channer Clinic (card no. 339), and later the Elders Nursing Home. It was demolished in 1960 and the site became a parking lot for the Pasteur Medical Building (card no. 343).

371. This home, the residence of Frank Coombs and his wife, Elizabeth, was at 115 Northwest Fourteenth Street. Note the attractive stained glass window at the left front corner of the house. Viewed from inside, this splash of color added immeasurably to the beauty of the home. While we are not certain, it seems possible that this scene may have been included in a builder's portfolio for advertising purposes. In 1914 Frank Coombs was a partner with H. S. Kramer in the Kramer-Coombs Coal and Material Company, located at 501 West Main. Some years ago this house was demolished and the site is now occupied by part of the St. Luke's United Methodist Church complex.

372. This fine home at 2201 Classen Boulevard, built in 1917, has experienced the same fate as many other houses constructed along Classen when it was strictly a residential street. The pattern has repeated itself many times: a few years as a private residence followed by conversion to a commercial establishment. In the 1940's, when this card was published, the building housed the Mutual Reserve Life Insurance Company. The architecture of the house is a style often seen in the older sections of the city, generally designated as "California bungalow," from its origins on the west coast. Today an insurance agency occupies the structure.

Brickwork by J. W. Bradburn, Oklahoma City.
Round Edge Vitrified Face Brick furnished – Cleveland Vit. Brick Co., Cleveland, Okla.
Herskowitz Residence, Oklahoma City.
Stewart & Wilderson, General Contractors, Oklahoma City.
370

Residence of Frank Coombs Oklahoma City Okla 115 N. W. 14th
371

372
HOME OF MUTUAL RESERVE LIFE COMPANY, 2201 CLASSEN BLVD.   WESBANCO OKLA. CITY.

NATIONAL TOURIST APARTMENTS OKLAHOMA CITY

373. "Strictly modern," the advertising boasted, when promoting the National Tourist Apartments in Oklahoma City in the mid-1930's. On U. S. Highway 77, the north and south highway through town, this facility was some 1¼ miles north of the State Capitol on Lincoln Boulevard. Sinclair brand gasoline was sold from pumps that permitted the buyer to see beforehand the exact amount of gasoline that would be gravity-fed into his gasoline tank. The vignette in the lower left of this view shows the wall heater inside the front door, as well as an extra blanket at the foot of the metal bed, provided just to make sure that the patron slept warm.

CAMP JACKSON ～ 3300 Lincoln Blvd. ～ Oklahoma City, Oklahoma

374. Camp Jackson was located at 3300 North Lincoln Boulevard, nine blocks north and "in the shadow of the State Capitol." This early view shows a Kerr's Barbecue on one side and a service station on the other, offering gasoline, lubricants, and tire repairs. Later, the name of the operation was changed to Jackson Courts, and the space that had formerly been the gas station was converted to additional overnight units. The Jackson Courts was known for its "$2.00 and up" room rent.

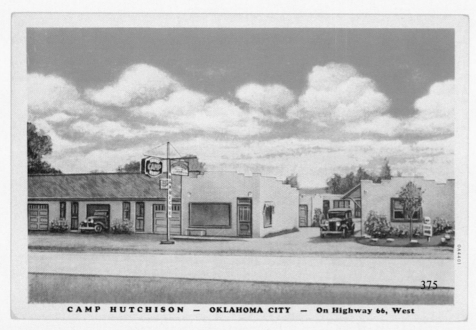

CAMP HUTCHISON — OKLAHOMA CITY — On Highway 66, West

375. "A place to get a good night's rest after a hard day's drive," was the motto used in advertising Camp Hutchinson. Since it ran through the heart of America east and west, Highway 66 was called "The Main Street of America," and it was on this highway in the twenty-one hundred block of Northwest Thirty-ninth Street that Camp Hutchinson was located. It had eating facilities and, like Camp Jackson, the owners were proud of their barbecue. All of the modern conveniences were offered to the traveler and undoubtedly this was a big improvement over camping out which had previously been the order of the day.

376. By 1923 automobile tourist traffic along the Postal Highway, later designated Route 66, had increased to the point that during the vacation season 150 cars were passing through Oklahoma City per day. Since there were no commercial tourist camps available, people were forced to rely on the city-provided facilities at Lincoln Park and the Lake Overholser dam. Community leaders began to call for the establishment of an official tourist park, and the following year (1924) saw the founding of the Log Cabin Tourist Park at Northwest Thirty-ninth and Altadena. This facility was to be a popular stopping place for tourists for some thirty years. Its advertising proclaimed, "The tourists are our travelling advertisement ... Fellowship treatment, pure water, oodles of shade, rest rooms — all free. Shower baths for the whole family, 25¢." Eventually cabins were added and even a movie theatre, the Log Cabin. Today a large apartment complex occupies the site.

377, 378. The Park-O-Tell complex in Oklahoma City was the first of a proposed chain of ten such units that were to be built north to Wichita and south to El Paso. **The Daily Oklahoman** called it a "Palace for Tourists" on opening day, Sunday, February 9, 1930. Completed at a cost of $185,000, the complex consisted of three Spanish-style buildings, facing east on Lincoln Boulevard, two blocks north of the State Capitol. There was a two-story hotel of sixty-eight rooms, along with a sixty-eight car garage; a coffee shop; and a gas station, which also housed a beauty parlor and barber shop. One patron remembered the convenience of "being in your room and snapping on the radio connection and listening to whatever the operator of the master set downstairs chose to bring in." There was also a special type of door used on the guest rooms. With a small knob the shutter could be regulated to permit air and light to enter the room without disturbing one's privacy. Velvety carpeting, a spacious lounge, and soundproofing between the bedrooms and the garage area, and later, sightseeing tours in a station wagon ... why, everything was "jake" at the Park-O-Tell!

376 THE OFFICIAL TOURIST PARK OF OKLAHOMA CITY
PLENTY SHADE, DEEP WELL WATER, SHOWERS, SEWERAGE, LIGHTS, CABINS, POLICED.

SEMINOLE AND KICKAPOO 1925 ANNUAL POW WOW

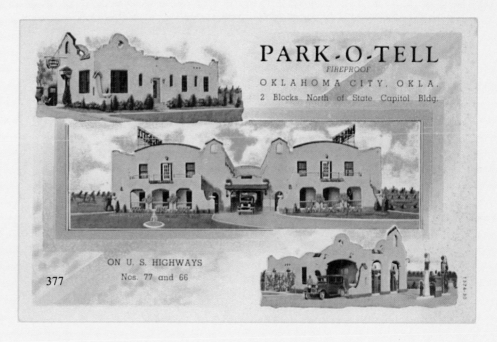

PARK-O-TELL
FIREPROOF
OKLAHOMA CITY, OKLA.
2 Blocks North of State Capitol Bldg.

377

ON U. S. HIGHWAYS
Nos. 77 and 66

PARK-O-TELL
Oklahoma City, Okla.
On U. S. Highways 66 and 77

"Daily Complimentary Sight -

Seeing Tours in our Station Wagon"

378

MATLYN COURT . . . U. S. 66 . . . Oklahoma City, Oklahoma

379

379. In the post-World War II years, Matlyn Court was found on the west side of Oklahoma City at 3520 Northwest Thirty-ninth Street, on U. S. Highway 66. The AAA recommendation had an impact on the tourist business and set standards that travelers were able to rely on for quality in all parts of the country. Matlyn Court had units that were air-conditioned in the summer and steam-heated in the winter. They also offered closed garages and modern tile showers. This court, and many of the others shown on these pages, represent "mom and pop" entrepreneurship, which was the forerunner to the contemporary nationwide chains which rule the highway today.

ONE OF THE MOST MODERN MOTEL COURTS IN THE SOUTHWEST
ON U. S. HIGHWAY 77
CORNER 44th STREET AND SOUTH ROBINSON—OKLAHOMA CITY

380

380. The Odom Annex Court at Forty-fourth and South Robinson, was, as its advertising suggested, "one of the most modern motel courts in the Southwest." Accommodations in every room included a telephone and radio, Beautyrest mattress and box springs, panel ray heating, and air conditioning for its patron's comfort. The sign in front showed rates of $3.00 and up. On the AAA list of recommended places to stay, the Odom Annex Court offered all the modern conveniences and comforts of home on the road.

Airline Motel

Oklahoma City, Okla.

381

381. The Airline Motel offered overnight units "near the Municipal Airport", even though it was located on Highways 62 and 277, several miles from the airport. In the 1950's this AAA member boasted suites as well as rooms "with all tile baths." This card drew attention to the location of the motel through its name and logo's being formed by the vapor trail of an airplane. This kind of visual name association has long proved a good marketing tool in promoting new and repeat business.

382. The Alamo Plaza Courts, at Forty-fourth and South Robinson, had its formal opening on September 6, 1936. Built of stucco in the Spanish style, there were thirty single rooms, and apartments with two to four rooms each. All bathrooms had shower and tub baths, tile floors and walls, and hot and cold running water. All apartments were completely furnished with linens, dishes, silverware and cooking utensils, and also had Stewart-Warner electric refrigerators and modern gas ranges. Each unit had its own individual garage. This early-day motel is still in business.

383. The Western Motel, whose sign, boasting a large cowboy hat, points with an arrow to the motel office, is on Highway 66, west of the city. At the time this postcard was issued, the motel had twenty-four units with tile baths, a tub and shower in every room, air conditioning by refrigeration, panel ray heating, and wall to wall carpeting. The motels shown on these pages span several decades of innovation and added comfort for travelers in Oklahoma City. The changes continue: black and white TV, followed by color and then cable; and the introduction of king-sized and water beds, swimming pools, and health studios. New highway systems, higher priced real estate, and the increasing amounts of capital needed to open a competitive motel have forced the "mom and pop" places out of existence and replaced them with conglomerates and big chains.

HIGHWAY 66 WEST — OKLAHOMA CITY, OKLAHOMA

384. Seen in this unusual view is the Clanton Trailer Park, located on busy Southeast Twenty-ninth Street in Oklahoma City. It is now surrounded by business and residential development, but when it was first established some thirty years ago, its location was secluded and rural. The park, with spaces for ninety-five small to medium-sized trailers, has remained under Clanton family management throughout its history. With its large shade trees, the Clanton Trailer Park is an attractive place to live, and its appearance is still very much like this old postcard scene.

CLANTON TRAILER PARK
5009 Southeast 29th Street — Oklahoma City, Oklahoma

385. This view shows the southeast corner of the Santa Fe depot which was situated west of the tracks that run north and south through the city. An elevated view of the entire depot may be examined in card no. 111. Torn down in 1930, the stones from the depot building were purchased and used to build the Oklahoma City Church of God at Northwest Tenth and Shartel in 1932. The stones from the central tower in the depot were numbered and then reconstructed as the church's bell tower.

386. This Moisant Monoplane was among several pioneer aeroplanes seen at the International Aviators' meet held at the Oklahoma City fairgrounds in mid-January, 1911. Quite a number of the "bird men" were there: the "fool flyer" Rene Simon, who flew a little Bleriot plane; and Rene Barrier, who, like Simon, delighted the audience with " a spectacular flight of altitude." **The Daily Oklahoman** reported that "Barrier might have been a would-be Arctic explorer to judge from his appearance when he landed his aeroplane in the field at the close of his flight. His carburetor was a mass of frost and his hands were encased in frost covered gloves. His face was blue from the cold and it was several moments after he had alighted, before he was able to speak."

387. The 89'er celebration has long been important to Oklahoma City folks, perhaps even more so in the early days, when so many of the participants were still around to recall when the Territory of Oklahoma was thrown open to public settlement. For several years this celebration was also the time of the Aprilis Fiesta. On April 21, 1911, Russell Pryor assumed the role of Rex Aprilla and is said to have "landed on the roof" of the Lee-Huckins Hotel in a Curtiss biplane and to have been greeted with a "twenty-one gun salute." Later in the day the "King" was given the key to the city by Mayor Daniel Lackey and honored by a parade. He was presented with a "Queen," and the royal couple, along with suitable attendants and flower girls, reigned proudly over a grand masked ball. This view shows the Rex just after he "landed on the roof!"

388. This enlarged postcard greeting was created to commemorate the first Air Mail Service into Oklahoma City on May 12, 1926. **The Daily Oklahoman** gave this stirring account: "At one minute past 3 o'clock, the Curtiss carrier pigeon became visible several miles away. It veered to the eastern side of the field, and then landed from the south, pulling up to the hanger at the northwestern corner, where fully 150 automobiles of spectators awaited it ... Here H. W. Parker, Oklahoma City manager of the National Air Transport company and C. B. McClelland, assistant superintendent of mails, climbed aboard and opened the mail compartment, to throw out the four sacks of mail dispatched to Oklahoma City. As the sacks were being unloaded, and others loaded, the fuel tank was refilled and soon the plane was racing across the field again to start the last leg of its journey." The southbound plane was piloted by R. L. Dobie, who wore a parachute folded so that he sat on it in the plane. If anything should happen, the jerk of a string would loosen it.

The cost of sending this postcard to Dallas was 10¢, to New York City, 15¢. Air Mail addressed to other cities went as far as possible by air, and then by rail to its destination.

388

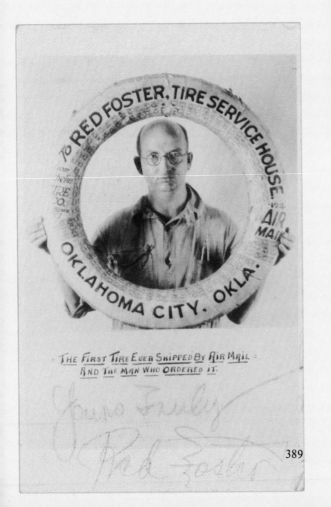

389

389. Red Foster must have been a swell guy. In an effort to give delivery on a new Michelin tire, he had the first tire ever shipped by Air Mail sent from New York City to Oklahoma City in 1926. The package weighed sixteen pounds and the stamps on the parcel totaled $39.00 in postage. The delivery time was seventeen and a half hours. Red was pleased with himself for having thought of this plan, so much so that he had a picture taken of the tire with himself in the center! Instead of being satisfied with one print for his office, he had others made into postcards and even autographed them for his customers and friends. Red's Tire Service House was at 119 South Robinson. Red Foster's ingenuity is certainly a tribute to private enterprise!

390. In 1941, the War Department announced its intention to build a centrally located maintenance and supply depot, and Oklahoma City was chosen for the site because of the availability of a large labor force. Construction began on land acquired by the city east of town, off Twenty-ninth Street. On March 1, 1942, the War Department activated the base as the Oklahoma City Air Depot, and by June, some 2,800 civilian employees were hired. In August, the Oklahoma City Chamber of Commerce asked the War Department to consider changing the name of the base to "Tinker Field" in honor of Major General Clarence L. Tinker, a native Oklahoman who had been killed on June 7, 1942 in a bombing raid on Wake Island. This request was granted, and the base officially became "Tinker Field" on October 14, 1942. Tinker continues to be important to our nation's defense and is the city's largest employer.

391. Wiley Post first distinguished himself and Oklahoma City in 1930 when he won the National Air Derby race from Los Angeles to Chicago. In this view, Post is shown with his plane, "The Winnie Mae," which was named for Mrs. Leslie Fain, daughter of Oklahoma City independent oil operator F. C. Hall, who employed Wiley Post in the late 1920's and early 1930's. In addition to his great flights, he is remembered as a pioneer in high altitude flight technology and for his development of clothing that enabled pilots to survive in the thin, cold air of higher altitudes. In July, 1933, he thrilled the world when he circled the globe in a record seven days, eighteen hours, and fifty minutes. The Oklahoma Historical Society (card no. 39) has on permanent display a large number of artifacts that document Wiley Post and his many achievements. Wiley Post and his passenger Will Rogers were killed in August, 1935, when their plane crashed near Point Barrow, Alaska.

392. In the Depression days it took considerable promotion to attract the financial backers needed to build suitable air facilities. As Roy Stewart tells in his book **Born Grown,** "A bond issue secured 640 acres for a new Municipal Airport, now the west section of Will Rogers World Airport, which began operation in 1932 with thirty-two daily inbound and outbound passenger and express schedules." This view shows the fine Art Deco structure that was constructed. Offering complete terminal service "to wayfarers of the air, the facility was said to be one of the finest fields in the country, and an easy twenty minute auto ride from the heart of Oklahoma City."

393, 394. The Municipal Field underwent a period of expansion and improvement in the late 1930's and into the next decade. The runways, which had previously been graveled, were paved and increased in numbers and length. The field's lighting was improved. Overall, many hundreds of thousands of dollars were spent to update the facility. Still more changes were made by mid-1941, when the airport was dedicated as the Will Rogers Air Base by the Army Air Corps. Will Rogers Field became a training base for light and heavy bombers, for photo reconnaissance, and for weather forecasting. Thousands of men were trained for World War II service as bomber crews, engineer companies, and other aspects of war work. Following the war, in the spring of 1946, Will Rogers Field was returned to the city for use as a civilian airport, once again permitting private air traffic to operate, along with the regularly scheduled airline flights.

Will Rogers Air Base, Oklahoma City, Okla.

395. The remodeling previously mentioned is apparent in this view of the tower facilities that were added to the older Municipal Air Terminal (card no. 392). Still another major renovation and expansion occurred in 1954. In early December, 1966, the present-day Will Rogers World Airport was dedicated and opened to air traffic. Its namesake, Will Rogers, is honored by the presence of a splendid bust, sculpted by Jo Davidson, who also created the full figure statue of Will Rogers in Claremore, Oklahoma. In recent years Oklahoma City has progressed into the space age and is dependent for much of its economic success on the air-related industries in the area.

Administration Building, Will Rogers Field, Oklahoma City, Okla.

Reinforced Concrete Arch Bridge Over the North Canadian River, Oklahoma City, Oklahoma. Built by The Topeka Bridge and Iron Co., Topeka, Kans.

396. Announcement of the planned construction of this new reinforced concrete arch bridge, to be located where Exchange Avenue crosses the North Canadian River, was made in **The Daily Oklahoman** on July 13, 1910. The cost was to be $55,000 and plans called for it to be sixty-seven feet wide, with sidewalks and a sixteen foot road on either side of double streetcar tracks down the center. The expense was to be shared among the county, park board, and the Oklahoma Railway Company. Construction was by The Topeka Bridge and Iron Co. of Topeka, Kansas, which came to Oklahoma City having just completed a bridge over the Arkansas River in Blackwell, Oklahoma. Sixty employees worked three shifts, night and day, to complete this bridge on April 1, 1911.

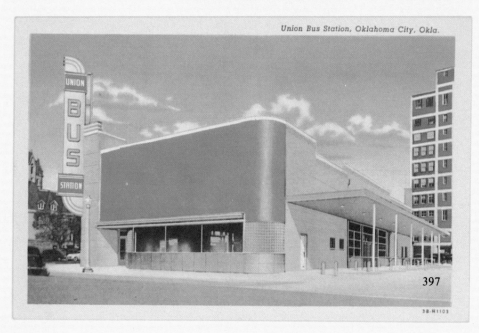

Union Bus Station, Oklahoma City, Okla.

397

397. As the highway systems improved, there was a gradual change from dependence on the railroads to other forms of public transportation, including the bus. In time, privately owned bus lines consolidated into larger regional and national firms that served urban and rural areas, transporting both goods and people to every part of the state. In 1941, a new $100,000 Union Bus Station was built on the northeast corner of Sheridan and Walker. Like many public buildings erected in the 1930's, this one incorporated Art Deco features in its design, making it an attractive reminder of an earlier time. Centrally located, it remains a busy facility.

398

398. Mr. T. T. Eason brought several firms together in the 1920's and formed the Eason Oil Company. By controlling exploration, production, refining, and marketing, the Eason Oil Company was able to expand and become a major competitor in the petroleum industry throughout Oklahoma and the midwest. During the Depression, a portion of the company's holdings had to be sold, and after the Enid refinery burned, Eason retrenched and stayed active only in the exploration and production aspects of the business. Now a part of the ITT conglomerate, the Eason Oil Company's offices are in the Oil Center Building on the Northwest Expressway. This circa 1930 view is believed to depict the company's facility at 2400 Northwest Thirty-ninth Street.

399. This is a view taken from the State Capitol building looking toward the northeast: Twenty-third Street runs east and west in front of the Capitol while Lincoln Boulevard extends north from the statehouse. With a strong magnifying glass one can detect that the white two-story house in the foreground has a sign reading "Emergency Hospital - McBride Clinic," and that a nurse is standing on the front porch. To the left is an oil derrick that is partially curtained with corrugated metal sheeting, a precaution for nearby property in case the well "blew." About a block north on Lincoln Boulevard, on the left, or west side of the street, the Park-O-Tell (card no. 377), almost surrounded by oil derricks, can be seen.

400. Nestled among fine homes near the Governor's mansion was the "Oklahoma City Mansion Pool." Four boilers generated the steam that drove the rotary rig drill. The size of all this oil well drilling equipment dwarfs the automobile in the lower right corner. Governor E. W. Marland defied Oklahoma City politicos by calling out the National Guard to assure that the oil men would be protected from city officials who attempted to deliver restraining orders. The Governor won his legal battle and the state retained control of drilling rights on its own property.

401. This striking night view shows the intensity with which the oil men worked; likewise, it gives an idea of how disruptive it must have been to the home owners who attempted to keep their property and live a normal life. The machinery, men, and all of the activity, together with the sounds and smells, associated with this kind of drilling and production, would have been either aggravating or pleasing depending on one's perspective, which was determined by the amount of financial gain either promised or dreamed possible. In their book **Early Oklahoma Oil** by Franks, Lambert, and Tyson, the authors stated "The Oklahoma City Field's high point of production was reached in 1933, when 66,985,000 barrels of crude oil were pumped from the pool's wells."

402. The photographer stood on the highest point of the roller coaster (card no. 173), not the carousel, as the mislabeled card states, aimed his camera north and captured what must be one of the finest overall views of the state fairgrounds. The carousel is the turreted, circular structure in the middle foreground, and the exposition building is easily seen in the distant right portion of the view. The midway, which extends along the west side of the walkway, is placed in perspective, and privately owned structures outside the fairgrounds are visible in the distance.

403. In the early days, the easiest way to get to the State Fair from town was to take the streetcar that followed Eighth Street to Eastern Avenue and the fairgrounds. By comparing this view with card no. 169, one can see that substantial improvements have been made, the most visible being the covered shed for the loading and unloading of streetcar passengers. The trolley wires above follow the curved trackway that winds in and out of the fairgrounds. A photographer stands near his camera and tripod on the left.

404. Spectators surrounded the racetrack the day that this photograph was taken, while others remained in their open carriages to enjoy the added elevation and shade. All eyes were on the horse race, and undoubtedly some money, too! The North Canadian River wound its way south and east of the fairgrounds and in 1923, 1926, and 1927, the river swept over the lowlands and transformed the racetrack and most of the surrounding area into a lake. The fairgounds location remained politically controversial for several more decades before it was moved permanently to the west side of town, at Northwest Tenth and May.

405. Shown here is one of Oklahoma City's earliest motion picture theatres, the Yale No. 2, located at 316 North Broadway. By 1908, the date of this card, several movie theatres were doing business in the city, including the Dreamland, the Gaiety, the Elite, and the Odeon. Other theatres were strictly vaudeville houses; while a third category combined the two forms of entertainment. A Yale advertisement from 1908 urged the reader to enjoy a "comfortable half hour in Oklahoma City's most magnificent motion picture theatre." The ad also promised that "the very finest films are used exclusively in this popular amusement house." Admission was a nickel.

406. Brothers John and Peter Sinopoulo bought the old Overholser Opera House (card no. 31) in 1917, and over the next few years rebuilt and transformed it into the Orpheum Theatre. Investing $500,000 in the project, they made many innovations, including a new seating arrangement with 1,040 seats in the auditorium and six boxes and twelve loges in the balcony area. The boxes and loges were all tastefully furnished with wicker furniture. There were no columns to obstruct patrons' views and the theatre was a "harmony of colors and design throughout." Opening night was January 26, 1921, with Ralph Dunbar's production of the comic opera classic, "The Mikado." Surely the Orpheum Theatre was the "Most Gorgeous Playhouse in The Southwest."

407. Following the Second World War, Americans' automobiles not only transported them to the movies, but became their theatre as well. Drive-in theatres began to sweep the nation and it is thought that the Northwest Highway Drive-In was the first to be built in Oklahoma City. This view shows the Skyview Drive-In, built soon after, on U. S. Highways 62 and 270, at 3800 Northeast Twenty-third Street. The Skyview provided space for 1,000 automobiles and the "ultimate in theatre entertainment." The population shift to the suburbs and rising land values have doomed many of the drive-ins in the Oklahoma City area, but the Skyview was built at the edge of town and survives to this day.

THE FAMOUS KILTIE BAND AT CIVIC CENTER, OKLAHOMA CITY

408. "Does your daughter drink or smoke?" This was the initial question that Captain E. G. Fry, organizer of the Kiltie Band, would ask the parents of a prospective new member. If the girl abstained from drink and tobacco, she had to be able to read music and be about the same size as the other girls, so that the uniforms would not have to be altered too often. If she met these qualifications, she was able to join a band which paid nothing, had practice every Saturday night, and also required members to be available for trips. The trips themselves entailed a lot of hard work — marching, playing, sore feet — but also were a lot of fun. Organized in 1922, first for the Yeomen, a fraternal insurance group, Capt. Fry's Kiltie Band became the grand promoter of Oklahoma City as it traveled for twenty-two years to every large city in the United States and Canada.

Oklahoma City Rangers

409. These Oklahoma City Rangers put on their red silk western shirts, mounted their horses, and participated in the Golden Jubilee Parade through downtown Oklahoma City on April 22, 1939. The big event was the Fiftieth Anniversary of Oklahoma City, and this round-up club helped to make it a grand celebration! The group participated in other civic events from time to time, and then disbanded.

Boat Docks on Lake Hefner, Oklahoma City, Oklahoma

410. The big reservoir northwest of Oklahoma City known as Lake Hefner became the home of the enthusiastic Oklahoma City Boat Club, Inc., around 1950, the approximate date of this scene. The club negotiated a lease with the city while construction at the lake was still in progress. A boat harbor appropriate for all types of pleasure craft, including sailboats, was dredged along the east shore. This sheltered anchorage area has attracted large numbers of sailing enthusiasts who enjoy pursuing their hobby in land-locked Oklahoma.

411. Springlake Park, located in a beautifully wooded area just west of Lincoln Park, was the dream of Roy Staton, who created this wonderland in the early 1920's. Almost from the beginning, the swimming pool shown here was a feature attraction, offering crystal-clear, semi-artesian well water. In the early days there were two pools side by side and while one was being cleaned and refilled the other was open to bathers. Eventually, the pools were combined into one unit as shown in this view. There was dancing for 10¢ at the Fairyland Ballroom, where patrons were treated to the strains of Hogan Hancock's Merrymakers, nine internationally famous musicians. A firefly crystal ball, hung above the center of the pavilion, added a special touch to moonlight dancing.

411

POOL AND PLAYGROUND — SPRINGLAKE AMUSEMENT PARK — OKLAHOMA CITY

PARTIAL VIEW   BIG DIPPER

412

SPRINGLAKE AMUSEMENT PARK — OKLAHOMA CITY

JUDY

413

412. Promotions of the roller coaster purported it to be "The most thrilling, breathtaking ride in the whole Southwest. We'll turn you white as a sheet and make you like it — yet, it's super safe. Finest equipment, finest engineering, you take no chances. And we know you'll like it." The park also featured a waffle house, with food prepared at reasonable prices, a juvenile railway, a pony track, a fun house, a shooting gallery, and numerous other amusements offering children and adults a good time. Roy Staton's son Marvin managed the park until its recent closing.

413. Hundreds of people, many of them children, contributed their nickels and dimes to raise $8,000 to buy a baby elephant for the Oklahoma City Zoo. Individuals mailed in name suggestions and "Judy" was the name finally chosen. Reporting on the parade which took place on May 21, 1949, when she was introduced to the city, **The Daily Oklahoman** said: "Old folks laughed, clapped and cheered, and kids screamed, grinned and bashfully turned their heads. One women held up a cocker dog to see the elephant, [and] a milk wagon horse shied and climbed a curb."

Leopard, Oklahoma City Zoo

414

414. A "metropolitan safari" was initiated after "Leapy" the leopard escaped from the Oklahoma City Zoo in Lincoln Park on February 25, 1950. Leapy jumped in a ricochet-like manner from the bottom of his eighteen-foot pit to the side, then to the top, and escaped. Amateur hunters with every imaginable type of weapon searched the park and surrounding area for three days, assisted by planes from the Civil Air Patrol, the Air National Guard, and a helicopter from Fort Sill. Reported sightings came from as far away as one hundred miles, but Leapy was discovered in a deep slumber near his pit, having eaten some drugged meat left by zoo workers. The shock of the drug and the stimulant administered to counteract it was too much and Leapy died, but not before publicizing Oklahoma City through nationwide news bulletins.

MONKEY ISLAND, LINCOLN PARK, OKLAHOMA CITY, OKLA.—75

415

415. "Monkey Island" is one of the most popular attractions at the Oklahoma City Zoo in Lincoln Park. The portholes, ropes, and ratlines on the simulated shipwreck offer a playground for the monkeys, whose antics are a constant delight to spectators. Much of the original part of the zoo, including this exhibit and the stone grotto animal enclosures, was constructed by the WPA during the 1930's.

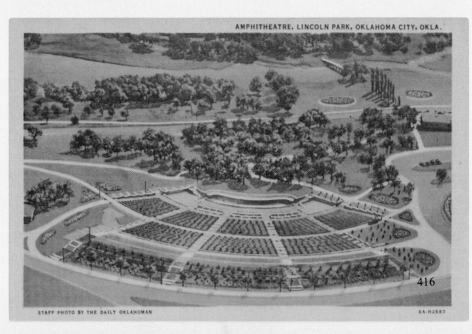

AMPHITHEATRE, LINCOLN PARK, OKLAHOMA CITY, OKLA.

416

STAFF PHOTO BY THE DAILY OKLAHOMAN   6A-H2687

416. The Civilian Conservation Corps built this amphitheatre in Lincoln Park. Native stone was used to construct a two-level stage and banks of seats in a huge, pie-shaped wedge. The amphitheatre has a gradual slope from the front to rear, permitting an unobstructed view of the stage from any seat in the facility. The architect's original drawings called for stone towers at either side of the stage, one to hold sound equipment and the other for lighting, but these were never built. The amphitheatre, which recently underwent a thorough renovation, has been the sight of countless varied performances over the years.

417. This view shows the Clara H. Girvin Bridge located in Lincoln Park. The bridge was dedicated on July 19, 1923 in honor of Clara Girvin and her contributions as a member of the Oklahoma City Park Board. Lincoln Park, consisting of five hundred and forty acres, is the home of the Oklahoma City Zoo and is a major recreational facility. This attractively landscaped and wooded area has long been a favorite picnic spot for area residents.

CLARA H. GIRVIN BRIDGE, LINCOLN PARK, OKLAHOMA CITY, OKLA.

418. The original Putnam Park (card no. 163) was later renamed Memorial Park in remembrance of the men and women who served in World War I. The park lies east of Classen Boulevard at Thirty-fourth Street. The twenty-foot fountain shown here was built in 1927 at a cost of $3,500. In the days before air conditioning, when more people took afternoon and evening walks, the fountain provided beauty, and was a focus of activity for children and adults in the neighborhood. Vandalism forced officials to turn off the water in 1941, and it was not until 1977, when the Uptown Kiwanis Club provided a portion of the funding, that the fountain was restored and once again made operational. Long forgotten, however, are original plans which called for a statue of a doughboy to be placed atop the structure.

MEMORIAL PARK FOUNTAIN AT NIGHT OKLAHOMA CITY, OKLAHOMA

419 This view of the conservatory in Wheeler Park (card no. 157) shows the greenhouse, seldom visited by the public, where bedding plants were nurtured and grown in a controlled environment for transplanting in this and other city parks. The walkways throughout the area were carefully maintained and bordered with seasonal flowers and shrubs. Located along the North Canadian River in the south part of Oklahoma City, much of Wheeler Park was destroyed in the "Great Flood" of 1923.

The authors from left to right:

Hal N. Ottaway (Post Office Box 18282, Wichita, Kansas 67218) operates an antiquarian book business and buys, sells, and appraises libraries, American Presidential materials, American Indian artifacts, photographs, and postcards. He is a 1976 graduate of the University of Oklahoma at Norman, with a PhD in anthropology.

Jim L. Edwards (311 South Klein, Oklahoma City, Oklahoma 73108) is the owner of the Abalache Book and Antique Shop. He specializes in Oklahoma state and local history, American Indian history, the Old West, and the Civil War in out-of-print books and related materials. Country-store signs, tins, and advertising items are other specialties of his shop. He attended the University of Oklahoma at Norman for two years, and graduated with a degree in history from Oklahoma Baptist University in Shawnee, Oklahoma.

ACKNOWLEDGEMENTS

Since the publication of **The Vanished Splendor,** we have been contacted by many collectors throughout the nation who brought to our attention additional views which they possessed. As we began to exchange information, it soon became obvious that there was enough new material available for another book of Oklahoma City postcards. The result, **The Vanished Splendor II,** would not have been possible, however, without the support of these collectors, who shared the images from their own collections. We are indebted to Ruth Slusher, Mrs. Virginia Alexander, Mitchell Oliphant, Don Nichols, Emma and Cecil Bridges, Mrs. C. S. Catlin, Kay and Max Stansbury, Dee Oburn, Hal Ross, Bert Jones, Frank Wood, Glenda Webster, Ed Hicks, Bill Hogan, John Dunning, Sally Postma, Sandy and John Millns, Kathy and Danny Danielsen, Andreas Brown, C. A. Morris, Kevin R. Johnson, Emily and Bill Waken, Susan Nicholson, Dixie Agnew, Fred Bright, and Dora and Don Ulrich..

While none of the featured businesses paid a fee to be included, we did call on a number of both present and past owners, managers, and employees, all of whom were generous in giving their time for interviews. We are appreciative of their assistance in providing information so that the descriptions would be as accurate as possible. Our thanks to Virgil Sprankle, Sam Oruch, J. G. Randall, Robert H. Lee, Mrs. Louise Dutcher, Clayton Anderson, Del Bowman, Raleine Wright, Frank Vater, Meta Soloyna, Tom Taggart, Mary Oliphant, Betty Brown, Johnny Meyers, Mrs. Naoma Smith, Laura Tucker, Cathy Conner, Bill E. Peavler, and the staff of the Oklahoma Historical Society library and microfilm room.

We are indebted to countless reporters who wrote about Oklahoma City before us, leaving a treasure trove in the newspaper files regarding occurrences which were reported as current events; also, to the historians who have carefully assembled materials for their articles, pamphlets, and books. We express our gratitude to Kent Ruth, Roy Stewart, Pendleton Woods, Mary Jo Nelson, Bob Blackburn, Kenny Franks, W. F. Kerr and Ina Gainer, the Oklahoma City Chamber of Commerce, George Shirk, Lucyl Shirk, Arn Henderson, and Melvena Thurman.

INDEX

MAIN STREET.   OKLAHOMA CITY, OKLA.